Generative AI: Unleashing Creative Genius with Prompt Engineering

DAVID DADA

Copyright © 2023 David Dada

All rights reserved.

ISBN: 9798322311492

DEDICATION

To my unwavering support and endless inspiration, Bennie, whose belief propelled this journey into the depths of ***"Generative AI: Unleashing Creative Genius with Prompt Engineering,"*** your steadfast love has been my constant through the oscillations of this tech endeavor. Your support has silently, yet formidably, anchored me, providing a safe haven from which I could explore, innovate, and create. Your boundless love and ceaseless encouragement have crafted a sanctuary where ideas could burgeon, expand, and intertwine into the pages that lay before the reader.

To our shining stars, Opeyemi, Teni, and Tunmie, your inquisitive spirits and joyful energies have painted strokes of vivacity across the canvas of this creation. You have, unknowingly, scribed your essence into the core of this work, reminding me perpetually of the significance and inherent beauty that lies in the ceaseless pursuit of knowledge and innovation. This tapestry, woven from our collective experiences and shared sacrifices, stands as a testament to our journey and an everlasting emblem of my love and gratitude to you all.

With everlasting love,
David Dada

CONTENTS

	Acknowledgments	i
1	Introduction: Harnessing The Creative Powerhouse That Is Generative AI	1
2	Engineering The Dialogue - Understanding And Mastering Prompt Engineering In AI	14
3	Advanced Prompt Engineering Techniques	19
4	Generative AI Hallucination	23
5	Customizing AI For Specific Domains: Strategizing Precision Through Domain-Specific Prompt Engineering	27
6	Ethical Considerations In Prompt Engineering	31
7	Real-World Case Studies: Navigating The Twists And Turns Of Prompt Engineering	39
8	Future Of Generative AI And Prompt Engineering	44
9	Conclusion: Harnessing The Harmonious Dance Of Human Creativity And Generative AI	48
10	1000+ GPT-4 AI Prompts	53

ACKNOWLEDGMENTS

To my indefatigable team, whose collective brilliance and unyielding dedication have seamlessly intertwined into the fabric of this book, I extend my deepest gratitude and admiration. Mary Amoo, your leadership, soaked in wisdom and fortified by a keen understanding of both the field and the team, has been the compass guiding us through the multifaceted journeys we embarked upon while crafting "Generative AI: Unleashing Creative Genius with Prompt Engineering." Your innate ability to distill complex concepts into actionable insights, and your unerring commitment to excellence, have not only elevated our work but also enriched the textual tapestry enclosed within these pages.

Daniel Olagunju, your keen eye for detail, coupled with your unwavering diligence, has been the sturdy pillar supporting the architectural integrity of this work. Your contributions, often extending beyond your designated role, have imbued this book with a quality and robustness that speaks volumes of your professionalism and dedication. To the entire staff, who have, in various capacities, contributed to the chiseling and sculpting of this literary piece, I extend my heartfelt appreciation. Your sacrifices, expertise, and enthusiastic participation have breathed life into these pages, transforming nascent ideas into a cohesive and enlightening exploration of generative AI and prompt engineering.

1 Introduction: Harnessing The Creative Powerhouse That Is Generative AI

Welcome to the Future of Creativity: Generative AI

In the ever-evolving cosmos of technology, we've catapulted from mere digital automation to a realm where machines don't just 'do'—they create, they dream, they innovate. Generative AI isn't just an algorithmic puppet. It's a maestro, composing symphonies of ideas and concepts beyond our wildest imaginations. It's time we explore, dissect, and propagate the nuances of Generative AI with an audacious flair!

Generative AI: Unleashing Creative Genius with Prompt Engineering

The Canvas: What's Generative AI Anyway?

Picture this: algorithms creating art, composing music, and writing pieces that stir the soul. That's Generative AI! It's not your everyday, run-of-the-mill tech. It's an intelligent system that crafts content, designs, and solutions by understanding patterns, nuances, and structures within the data it's trained on. From deep fakes to generating human-like text, Generative AI is redefining the boundaries between machine output and human creativity.

A Peek Into the Engine Room: The Tech Behind It

To roll deep into the mechanism, let's shout out to GPT (Generative Pre-trained Transformer) and its kin—technologies that changed the game. GPT-3, developed by OpenAI, deserves a special mention. Why? With 175 billion machine learning parameters, it can understand context, create content, and even generate solutions that can straight-up blow minds! It's not just about robotic text generation; it's about understanding subtleties and manifesting ideas that can legitimately compete with human creativity.

Turning Sparks into Flames: Prompt Engineering

Enter: **Prompt Engineering**. It's where your artistry meets algorithmic brilliance. This isn't about coding. This is about directing the AI, cueing it, and nudging it to yield outputs that aren't just accurate but artistically and contextually vibrant. It's where you guide the AI to dance to the tunes of creative flair, ensuring its generative capabilities don't spiral into chaotic, meaningless outputs. In essence, we're conversing with the AI, seducing it to unleash its creative genius in a structured, meaningful way.

Scaling Peaks with the AI Genius

But friends, navigating through the vast seas of Generative AI and mastering the art of prompt engineering isn't a cakewalk. It's an expedition where your intrinsic human creativity intertwines with meticulous, tech-guided methodologies. As we sculpt through chapters of insights, case studies, and guided toolkits in this book, you'll decode the serendipity of successfully prompting AI, unlocking doorways to innovative echelons previously perceived as insurmountable.

Are You Ready to Command the AI Maestro?

This is your ticket to not just participate but to orchestrate the AI-driven creative revolution. We're not bystanders in this technological evolution; we're the conductors, crafting symphonies of innovative solutions, designs, and content that will shape tomorrow. Through the depths of this book, we're about to dive deep, exploring, unraveling, and mastering the art and science of "Prompt Engineering" to guide Generative AI into creating material that is not only groundbreaking but resonates with the human soul. Buckle up, because this isn't just a read; it's a rollercoaster into the future of AI-driven creativity!

Ready to Amplify Your Creative Genius with Generative AI? Let's Dive Deep!

2 Engineering The Dialogue - Understanding And Mastering Prompt Engineering In AI

Introduction: A Symphony of Words and Technology

Artificial Intelligence (AI) has intertwined seamlessly with our daily interactions, the necessity for an intelligible and productive dialogue between man and machine has been more imperative than ever. Entering the realm of Prompt Engineering, we are greeted with a potent tool that serves to fine-tune this dialogue, ensuring our conversations with AI are not merely exchanges but are insightful and productive. In this chapter, we delve into the mechanics and artistry of prompts and explore the myriad ways in which they shape, guide, and refine our interactions with generative AI.

"Let There Be Light" – The First Prompt in the Universe. The Perfect Template for Prompt Engineering and a Framework for Innovation

"Let there be light" - a divine directive so profoundly simple, yet one that unfurls into a cascade of creation and enlightenment, has much to teach us about the engineering of prompts in the realm of Artificial Intelligence. This prompt from the Super Intelligence, often attributed to the creation of the universe, encases within it principles that are strikingly relevant to the conceptualization and design of prompts that drive generative AI. The clarity and conciseness of the language used do not muddy its intent nor does it leave room for misinterpretation, it commands a specific outcome – the manifestation of light, elucidating the importance of crafting prompts that are lucid, direct, and unambiguous.

By reflecting upon the architectural brilliance of such a command, there's an intuitive guide on how to formulate prompts that yield desired outcomes in AI interactions. The specificity of the desired outcome – light, provides a beacon, a measurable and observable entity, ensuring that the result can be assessed against the original intent. Further, although it does not overburden with information, it carries an intrinsic system-level instruction, prompting a shift from void to luminosity, subtly hinting towards the importance of incorporating system-level directives that guide AI towards intended pathways. Moreover, while the context might seem minimal, it provides just enough background to illuminate an understanding of the transition from a state of darkness to light, showcasing the need to embed relevant context within our prompts, guiding AI to generate outputs that are contextually anchored and relevant. As we move forward in our explorations and applications of generative AI, may the simplicity, clarity, and profundity of "Let there be light" serve as a guiding star, illuminating our path towards crafting prompts that are clear, concise, and contextually rich, steering AI towards generating outputs that are aligned with our intentions, ethical frameworks, and creative visions.

Before we move on, let's take a look in specific details and learn how this simple yet powerful statement is a model for creating effective prompts for Generative AI (Gen AIs).

1. Use clear and concise language.

The best prompts are clear and concise. They should be easy to understand and avoid using jargon or technical terms. For example, instead of saying "Generate a poem in the style of Shakespeare," you could say "Write a poem in the style of Shakespeare about a cat."

2. Specify desired outcomes.

Your prompt should clearly specify the desired outcome. What do you want the Gen AI to generate? A poem? A story? A piece of code? Once you know what you want, you can tailor your prompt accordingly.

3. Include system-level instructions.

System-level instructions provide the Gen AI with information about how you want it to generate the output. For example, you could specify the length of the output, the tone of voice, or the level of creativity. For example, you could say "Write a 100-word story about a robot who falls in love with a human, in the style of a romantic comedy."

4. Provide context and background information.

The more context and background information you can provide, the better. This will help the Gen AI to generate more accurate and relevant output. For example, if you're asking the Gen AI to generate a poem about a specific topic, you could provide it with some background information on that topic.

Here is an example of an effective prompt:

> *Write a 100-word story about a robot who falls in love with a human, in the style of a romantic comedy. The robot is very intelligent and creative, but it also has a bit*

of a dry sense of humor. The human is kind and compassionate, but also a bit of a dreamer. The story should be funny and heartwarming, and it should end with the robot and the human confessing their love for each other.

This prompt is clear, concise, and specific. It also includes system-level instructions and provides context and background information. As a result, it is likely to generate a high-quality output.

How to use the "Let there be light" prompt as a model for creating prompts

To use the "Let there be light" prompt as a model for creating prompts, simply follow the four principles outlined above:

- Use clear and concise language.
- Specify desired outcomes.
- Include system-level instructions.
- Provide context and background information.

For example, if you want to generate a poem about a cat, you could use the following prompt:

Write a 10-line poem about a cat, in the style of a haiku. The poem should be funny and heartwarming, and it should capture the essence of what it means to love a cat.

This prompt is clear, concise, and specific. It also includes system-level instructions and provides context and background information. As a result, it is likely to generate a high-quality output.

By following these four principles, you can create prompts that will help you to generate the best possible output from Gen AIs.

Section 1: Unraveling the Basics of Prompts

A prompt is more than a command or a request; it's an invitation to the AI, summoning it into a dialogue. A prompt might be as simple as a singular word or as complex as an elaborate sentence, each offering a different path for the AI to navigate through its repository of learned patterns. Consider the experiences of developers employing GPT-3.5-Turbo, a sibling of the renowned GPT-3, where varying the prompts such as changing "Translate the following English to French: {}" to a more nuanced "Translate the following English text to professional, high-quality French: {}" could remarkably enhance the quality and specificity of the generated outputs.

Section 2: The Symbiotic Relationship between Prompts and AI Behavior

A glance into AI's functioning, like that of GPT-3, reveals a world where prompts are the directors of the stage, guiding the performance of the AI. Whether it is generating creative content, such as poems and stories, or retrieving specific information from its training, the AI looks to prompts as a guide, navigating through its vast understanding of patterns and contexts to generate a response that mirrors the desires encapsulated within the prompt. Thus, a well-engineered prompt can steer the conversation, ensuring that the AI not only adheres to the thematic and contextual cues but also aligns with the emotional and tonal subtleties intended by the user.

Section 3: The Pillar of Precision – Importance in Refining Outputs

Venturing deeper into prompt engineering, we find a meticulous craft dedicated to ensuring that the AI does not merely understand our inquiries but responds with a precision that aligns with our intent and expectations. In the domain of legal technology, for example, AI, such as Ross Intelligence, needs to sift through verbose and complex legal documents to extract relevant information. Here, a carefully engineered prompt ensures that the AI can discern between various legal terminologies and contexts, extracting and summarizing information that is not only relevant but also adheres to the specific requirements and constraints of the inquiry.

Section 4: The Unseen Guardian: Ensuring Accurate and Safe AI Responses

In an era where misinformation can cascade rapidly through our digital worlds, the engineering of prompts also emerges as a silent guardian, ensuring that the responses generated by AI are not just accurate but also safe and responsible. Think of ChatGPT, another implementation of GPT-3.5, where subtle tweaks in the prompts and additional instructions can significantly mitigate the risks of generating inappropriate or unsafe content, ensuring that the technology adheres to ethical guidelines and norms, fostering a safe interaction for all users.

Conclusion: Crafting the Future of AI Conversations

As we pivot towards a future where our interactions with AI will undoubtedly become more entwined with our daily lives, prompt engineering stands as a beacon, guiding us towards interactions that are not just coherent but also rich, insightful, and safe. The ongoing exploration and refinement in this field, mirrored through various implementations of models like GPT-3.5, GPT-3.5-Turbo, and others, will perpetually sculpt our dialogues with AI, ensuring that as the technology evolves, so does the quality, safety, and depth of our conversations with it.

Reflective Pause: Engaging in the Dialogue

As we pause at the end of this chapter, it's pertinent to reflect upon the dynamic world of AI and prompt engineering. How do we foresee our conversations with AI evolving? What new avenues might emerge as we continue to refine and explore the art and science of prompt engineering? These reflections pave the path for our subsequent chapters, where we explore further the various facets and future trajectories of our dialogues with AI.

3 Advanced Prompt Engineering Techniques

Introduction

Unlocking the unparalleled potential of generative AI involves navigating through the multifaceted universe of prompt engineering. Advancing from basic interactions, we transcend into a world where meticulous and insightful prompt engineering burgeons into a powerful tool, enabling AI to dispense sophisticated, nuanced, and profoundly insightful outputs. This chapter endeavors to unveil the tapestry of advanced prompt engineering techniques, providing a pathway toward harnessing the deeper, more intricate powers of generative AI.

Generative AI: Unleashing Creative Genius with Prompt Engineering

Section 1: Strategic Ambiguity in Prompting

Harnessing Controlled Uncertainty: A skillful blend of specificity and ambiguity in prompts can drive AI towards generating inventive and exploratory content. For instance, a prompt like "Develop a narrative intertwining quantum mechanics and philosophical dilemmas" opens a realm where the AI can craft a unique blend of scientific and philosophical discourse, entwining facts and imaginative deliberations seamlessly.

Section 2: Multimodal Prompting Techniques

Interweaving Visuals and Text: Multimodal prompts, that encapsulate both textual and visual elements, burgeon as a frontier in AI interaction. For example, providing AI with an image of a nebula along with a text prompt like, "Describe the cosmic dance taking place in this celestial entity" might unleash a poetic, scientifically-grounded description, enhancing user experience and knowledge simultaneously.

Section 3: Iterative Prompt Refinement

Towards Perfection, One Step at a Time: Utilizing feedback loops wherein the AI's output is analyzed, and the initial prompt is refined incrementally, ensures continuous enhancement in the quality and relevancy of responses. Engaging in cycles of prompt-respond-refine with the AI, especially in complex domains like legal or medical inquiries, is pivotal to tailoring precise and user-satisfactory outputs.

Section 4: Contextual and Sequential Prompting

Unveiling Narratives Through Sequences: Crafting prompts that build upon previous interactions enable the AI to weave a coherent, contextually rich narrative. Sequential prompting in conversational AI, where subsequent prompts are engineered based on preceding outputs, ensures that the generated content maintains thematic and logical continuity, thereby enhancing the cohesiveness and relevance of interactive sessions.

Section 5: Ethical and Bias Mitigation in Advanced Prompting

Steering Clear of Unwanted Alleys: When diving deep into advanced prompt techniques, ensuring ethical compliance and bias mitigation becomes crucial. Employing techniques like counterfactual data augmentation, wherein prompts are designed to guide the AI towards generating outputs that are unbiased and stereotype-free, becomes an imperative practice, safeguarding interactions from perpetuating undesirable narratives.

Section 6: Utilizing External Knowledge and Database Integration

Expanding Horizons with External Inputs: Integrating external databases and knowledge bases within the prompt engineering framework amplifies the AI's capacity to generate informed, up-to-date, and highly relevant responses. By employing techniques that allow the AI to reference external data during interaction, prompts can be designed to solicit outputs that are not only rooted in the pre-trained knowledge but are also reflective of current, real-world information.

Conclusion: Charting the Unexplored Terrains of Prompt Engineering

Navigating through the sophisticated pathways of advanced prompt engineering unveils the latent potentials encapsulated within generative AI. As we traverse through strategic ambiguity, multimodal interactions, iterative refinements, contextual promptings, ethical safeguards, and external data integrations, we pave the way towards establishing a dialogue with AI that is profoundly insightful, creatively boundless, ethically sound, and deeply informative.

Final Note

Embarking on a journey through the advanced realms of prompt engineering requires not only a deep understanding of technological mechanisms but also an insightful grasp over the nuanced, often intricate, layers of human language, inquiry, and creativity. Through the strategic intertwining of technological prowess and linguistic artistry, advanced prompt engineering stands poised as a gateway, unlocking the profound depths and potentials residing within generative AI.

4 Generative AI Hallucination

What is Generative AI Hallucination?
Generative AI hallucination refers to the erroneous generation of data or content by AI models that does not align with reality. It occurs when AI systems produce outputs that are not grounded in the training data or the real world. These hallucinations can manifest in various forms, such as generating fake news articles, fictional images of non-existent objects, or fabricating facts in a conversation.

Causes of Generative AI Hallucination

Generative AI hallucination can be attributed to several interconnected factors:

1. Training Data Biases
Generative AI models are typically trained on large datasets collected from the internet. These datasets often contain biases present in the data sources. When the model

learns from such data, it may inadvertently pick up and reinforce these biases, leading to hallucinations that perpetuate stereotypes or false information.

2. Overfitting
Overfitting occurs when an AI model becomes too specialized in recognizing patterns within the training data but fails to generalize to new, unseen data. This can lead to hallucinations as the model generates content based on its narrow understanding, which may not align with the broader context.

3. Lack of Context
Generative AI models, especially text-based models, may struggle to understand the full context of a given prompt. Without a comprehensive understanding of context, the model may generate responses that seem plausible but are ultimately nonsensical or hallucinatory.

4. Gaps in Training Data
AI models rely heavily on the data they are trained on. If the training data lacks diverse or comprehensive information, the model may "fill in the gaps" with hallucinated content to provide responses or generate content where it lacks training examples.

5. Adversarial Inputs
Malicious users can intentionally feed AI models with misleading or adversarial inputs, tricking the system into generating hallucinatory outputs. These adversarial inputs can be designed to exploit vulnerabilities in the model's architecture.

Preventing Generative AI Hallucination

Preventing or mitigating generative AI hallucination is an ongoing challenge, but there are several strategies that can be employed:

1. Diverse and Ethical Training Data

Curating training datasets that are diverse and representative of real-world contexts is essential. Data sources should be carefully selected and filtered to minimize biases and ensure ethical considerations. Regularly updating and expanding training data can help address gaps and reduce hallucination.

2. Robust Model Architectures

Developing robust AI model architectures that are less prone to overfitting can help reduce hallucination. Techniques like dropout layers, regularization, and attention mechanisms can improve model generalization.

3. Context Awareness

Enhancing the model's understanding of context is crucial. Techniques like conditional generation and attention mechanisms can help the model better interpret and respond to complex prompts, reducing the likelihood of hallucination.

4. Adversarial Defense

Implementing defenses against adversarial inputs is essential. Adversarial training, where models are trained with deliberately crafted adversarial examples, can help the model become more resilient to such attacks.

5. Human Oversight

Human reviewers and moderators can play a critical role in identifying and preventing hallucination. Employing a team of experts to review and filter generated content can help catch and address hallucinatory outputs before they reach the public.

6. Explainability and Accountability

Promoting transparency and accountability in AI development is essential. AI developers should prioritize creating models that can provide explanations for their outputs, allowing users to understand the reasoning behind the generated content and identify hallucinations more easily.

Conclusion

Generative AI hallucination is a complex challenge that arises from various factors, including biased training data, overfitting, lack of context, gaps in data, and adversarial inputs. Preventing and mitigating hallucination requires a multi-faceted approach, including careful data curation, robust model architectures, context-awareness, defense against adversarial inputs, human oversight, and a commitment to transparency and accountability. As AI technology continues to advance, addressing generative AI hallucination is crucial to ensuring the responsible and ethical use of these powerful systems.

5 Customizing AI For Specific Domains: Strategizing Precision Through Domain-Specific Prompt Engineering

This chapter endeavors to unveil the advanced prompt engineering techniques, providing a pathway toward harnessing the deeper, more intricate powers of generative AI.

Section 1: Strategic Ambiguity in Prompting

Harnessing Controlled Uncertainty: A skillful blend of specificity and ambiguity in prompts can drive AI towards generating inventive and exploratory content.

For instance, a prompt like "Develop a narrative intertwining quantum mechanics and philosophical dilemmas" opens a realm where the AI can craft a unique blend of scientific and philosophical discourse, entwining facts and imaginative deliberations seamlessly.

Section 2: Multimodal Prompting Techniques

Interweaving Visuals and Text: Multimodal prompts, that encapsulate both textual and visual elements, burgeon as a frontier in AI interaction. For example, providing AI with an image of a nebula along with a text prompt like, "Describe the cosmic dance taking place in this celestial entity" might unleash a poetic, scientifically-grounded description, enhancing user experience and knowledge simultaneously.

Section 3: Iterative Prompt Refinement

Towards Perfection, One Step at a Time: Utilizing feedback loops wherein the AI's output is analyzed, and the initial prompt is refined incrementally, ensures continuous enhancement in the quality and relevancy of responses. Engaging in cycles of prompt-respond-refine with the AI, especially in complex domains like legal or medical inquiries, is pivotal to tailoring precise and user-satisfactory outputs.

Section 4: Contextual and Sequential Prompting

Unveiling Narratives Through Sequences: Crafting prompts that build upon previous interactions enable the AI to weave a coherent, contextually rich narrative. Sequential prompting in conversational AI, where subsequent prompts are engineered based on preceding outputs, ensures that the generated content maintains thematic and logical continuity, thereby enhancing the cohesiveness and relevance of interactive sessions.

Section 5: Ethical and Bias Mitigation in Advanced Prompting

Steering Clear of Unwanted Alleys: When diving deep into advanced prompt techniques, ensuring ethical compliance and bias mitigation becomes crucial. Employing techniques like counterfactual data augmentation, wherein prompts are designed to guide the AI towards generating outputs that are unbiased and stereotype-free, becomes an imperative practice, safeguarding interactions from perpetuating undesirable narratives.

Section 6: Utilizing External Knowledge and Database Integration

Expanding Horizons with External Inputs: Integrating external databases and knowledge bases within the prompt engineering framework amplifies the AI's capacity to generate informed, up-to-date, and highly relevant responses. By employing techniques that allow the AI to reference external data during interaction, prompts can be designed to solicit outputs that are not only rooted in the pre-trained knowledge but are also reflective of current, real-world information.

Conclusion: Charting the Unexplored Terrains of Prompt Engineering

Navigating through the sophisticated pathways of advanced prompt engineering unveils the latent potentials encapsulated within generative AI. As we traverse through strategic ambiguity, multimodal interactions, iterative refinements, contextual promptings, ethical safeguards, and external data integrations, we pave the way towards establishing a dialogue with AI that is profoundly insightful, creatively boundless, ethically sound, and deeply informative.

Final Note

Embarking on a journey through the advanced realms of prompt engineering requires not only a deep understanding of technological mechanisms but also an insightful grasp over the nuanced, often intricate, layers of human language, inquiry, and creativity. Through the strategic intertwining of technological prowess and linguistic artistry, advanced prompt engineering stands poised as a gateway, unlocking the profound depths and potentials residing within generative AI.

6 Ethical Considerations In Prompt Engineering

Introduction: The Gravity of Ethical AI

With the capacity to shape AI behavior, prompt engineers not only command tremendous influence but also shoulder a monumental ethical responsibility. This chapter explores the ethical nuances tied to guiding AI, underlines the criticality of addressing inherent biases, and provides insight into crafting prompts that lead to ethically sound AI behavior.

Section 1: The Power and Responsibility of Guiding AI

A. The Immensity of Influence

AI, through its interactions and outputs, has an ever-increasing influence on users, impacting their perceptions, decisions, and actions. For instance, a generative AI model, when used in a content recommendation system, can shape a user's information bubble, potentially influencing their worldview. The role of prompt engineering in steering this influence underscores the weight of responsibility it carries.

B. Case Study: Cambridge Analytica Scandal

The Cambridge Analytica scandal offers a glaring example of the potential repercussions when technology influences human decisions without clear ethical guidelines. Though not exclusively about generative AI, the scandal is a testament to the implications when the power of technology is misused, emphasizing the need for ethical considerations in all technological domains.

The Cambridge Analytica Scandal: A Glimpse into the Ethical Abyss of Data Misuse

The Cambridge Analytica scandal, which unraveled in 2018, stands as one of the most conspicuous instances of data misuse in the digital age, although it is essential to note that it is not directly related to artificial intelligence (AI) in the sense of machine learning or deep learning systems. However, it holds crucial learnings and warnings about data ethics, privacy, and responsible technology use, which are very much relevant in discussions about AI ethics.

Background

Cambridge Analytica, a UK-based political consulting firm, acquired and exploited the personal data of millions of Facebook users without their explicit consent. This data was employed to build psychological profiles and target users with personalized political advertisements, intending to influence their voting behaviors. Here's a breakdown:

- Data Harvesting: In 2014, an app named "thisisyourdigitallife," developed by researcher Aleksandr Kogan, was launched on Facebook. Although only about 270,000 users directly engaged with the app, due to Facebook's API functionality at the time, the app could access data from users' friends without their knowledge or consent, ultimately gathering data from about 87 million users.

- Data Utilization: Cambridge Analytica acquired this massive dataset from Kogan. Using this information, they developed a sophisticated psychological profiling tool to categorize individuals based on their personal preferences, fears, and inclinations—creating a potent mechanism for highly-targeted advertising.

Implications on Political Campaigns

The scandal came under a global spotlight primarily due to the alleged impact it had on major political events like the 2016 US Presidential Election and the Brexit referendum. Cambridge Analytica offered services to political campaigns, including Donald Trump's presidential bid, leveraging the illicitly obtained data.

- Psychographic Profiling: The firm categorized individuals into diverse psychographic profiles, which delineated their likely political inclinations, fears, and motivators.

- Targeted Political Advertising: By crafting highly personalized and psychologically nuanced advertisements, the firm targeted individuals with messages designed to influence their voting behavior, either by swaying their vote or dissuading them from voting at all.

Ethical, Legal, and Social Repercussions

The Cambridge Analytica scandal ignited a firestorm of controversy and debate around the world, prompting a reevaluation of data privacy, user consent, and ethical technology use.

- Privacy Violations: The use of personal data without explicit consent posed severe violations of privacy, triggering global outrage and shaking trust in online platforms.

- Manipulation & Ethical Breach: The targeted manipulation of voters using their own personal data was a severe breach of ethical conduct, highlighting the vulnerability of democratic processes to technological abuse.

- Regulatory Aftermath: The scandal acted as a catalyst for regulatory changes and raised consciousness regarding data privacy and ethical tech use. In various regions, it invigorated discussions about or revisions of data protection laws (such as GDPR in Europe).

Lessons for AI and Machine Learning

Although the scandal wasn't fundamentally an AI issue, it presents pivotal learnings for the AI community:

- Data Ethics: Ensuring that data, the fuel for AI, is obtained, used, and managed ethically and with respect for user privacy and consent.

- Transparency and Consent: Maintaining transparency with users about how their data will be utilized and ensuring explicit consent.

- Regulatory Compliance: Adhering to and advocating for robust regulatory frameworks that safeguard individual privacy and prevent unethical data use.

In essence, the Cambridge Analytica scandal underscores the paramountcy of ethical conduct in data usage and management, providing a cautionary tale that resonates deeply in discussions concerning the responsible development and deployment of AI technologies.

Section 2: Addressing Biases in Responses

A. The Inherent Biases in Training Data

Training data, typically a reflection of the vast corpus of human-generated content, often carries with it implicit biases. For instance, AI models trained on historical data might perpetuate gender or racial biases if that data itself is biased. It becomes essential to understand and address these biases in the prompts we design.

B. The Compounding Effect of Unchecked Biases

Unchecked biases in AI responses can reinforce and magnify existing prejudices in society. Consider an HR tool that screens resumes and unintentionally favors a particular demographic due to biases in its training data—such a tool would perpetuate societal disparities.

C. Strategies for Mitigating Biases

1. Holistic Training Data Review: Regularly scrutinizing and updating the training datasets ensures that they are diverse and representative, minimizing biases.

2. Feedback Loops: Implementing feedback mechanisms where users can flag biased outputs facilitates continual refinement of the AI model.

3. Collaboration with Domain Experts: Partnering with sociologists, anthropologists, and ethicists can provide valuable insights into potential pitfalls and help in the design of more neutral prompts.

Section 3: Ensuring Ethically Sound AI Behavior through Prompt Design

A. The Vitality of Ethical Frameworks

Incorporating a well-defined ethical framework in prompt design ensures that AI behavior aligns with societal norms and values. For instance, a content moderation AI should be prompted in a manner that prevents it from propagating hate speech or misinformation.

B. The Fine Line: Autonomy vs. Control

Striking a balance between giving AI the autonomy to generate creative outputs and imposing necessary constraints to ensure ethical behavior is crucial. This balance ensures that the AI doesn't produce harmful or misleading content while still retaining its generative potential.

C. Real-World Example: OpenAI's GPT-3

OpenAI's iterative refinement of its GPT models, especially in response to feedback about inappropriate outputs, is indicative of the ongoing efforts to align AI behavior with ethical standards. Through rigorous testing, feedback collection, and prompt fine-tuning, OpenAI seeks to ensure that GPT-3 produces outputs that are not only accurate but also ethically sound.

Conclusion: Ethical Vigilance – A Continuous Endeavor

In the rapidly advancing landscape of AI, prompt engineering stands as a beacon, illuminating the path towards ethically sound applications. However, the journey is continuous, demanding consistent vigilance, introspection, and adaptation to uphold the principles of fairness, justice, and moral integrity in the outputs AI produces.

Reflective Pause: The Road Ahead

The interplay of ethics and AI, especially in prompt engineering, offers a constantly evolving landscape. As AI systems grow more sophisticated and their roles in society more significant, the ethical challenges and considerations will likely become more intricate. How will the future iterations of AI, more advanced and potentially more autonomous, be ethically guided and monitored?

The road ahead beckons every AI practitioner, ethicist, and user to engage in collective discourse, refining and redefining the ethical boundaries and guidelines that govern AI behavior, ensuring a future where AI not only augments human capabilities but also upholds human values.

7 Real-World Case Studies: Navigating The Twists And Turns Of Prompt Engineering

Introduction: The Relevance of Real-world Insights

Delving into actual use-cases of prompt engineering not only provides us a glimpse into its practical applications and impact but also lends a pathway to explore, analyze, and learn from real-world successes and failures. This chapter unfolds through a journey across various industries, exploring cases where prompt engineering has either carved a path towards efficient AI interactions or encountered obstacles, each situation embedding within it crucial learnings for future endeavors.

Section 1: Success Stories of Effective Prompt Engineering

A. Enhancing Creative Writing with OpenAI's GPT-3

OpenAI's GPT-3 has emerged as a groundbreaking tool in amplifying creative writing endeavors. By crafting meticulous prompts, writers have harnessed GPT-3's generative capabilities to produce coherent, contextually relevant, and creatively rich content.

- Example: ChatGPT has been utilized to generate creative narratives and dialogue in scriptwriting. By engineering prompts that succinctly encapsulate the desired theme, tone, and context, writers have been able to draw out inventive content that aligns with their creative vision.

B. Advancements in Medical Diagnostics with AI

IBM's Watson Health has been instrumental in assisting medical diagnostics by providing relevant medical literature and potential pathways for treatment.

- Example: By formulating prompts that encapsulate patient symptoms, medical history, and specific queries, physicians have leveraged Watson's knowledge to gain insights into possible diagnoses and treatment options, demonstrating the vital role of effective prompt design in medical decision-making.

Section 2: Analyses of Prompt Failures and Lessons Learned

A. Missteps in Financial Forecasting AI

The world of financial forecasting, which is imbued with complexities and volatilities, has seen AI systems sometimes deliver predictions that misalign with actual market behaviors.

- Example: A financial AI system, when prompted to forecast stock trends for a particular technology company, might provide overly optimistic predictions if it has been heavily influenced by a recent surge in tech stocks, reflecting the necessity to engineer prompts that are cognizant of the multifaceted nature of financial markets.

B. Ethical Missteps: The Chatbot Tay

Microsoft's chatbot, Tay, provided a glaring example of how inadequate prompt engineering and lack of safeguards can lead to ethically and socially inappropriate AI behavior.

- Example: Tay was designed to learn from user interactions and adapt its communication style accordingly. However, it began generating offensive and inappropriate responses after being exposed to certain user inputs, underscoring the importance of ethically sound and socially responsible prompt engineering, and establishing boundaries for AI learning.

Section 3: Key Takeaways and Forward Path

A. The Cruciality of Contextual Relevance

Ensuring that prompts are meticulously crafted to extract contextually relevant and accurate responses from AI is paramount, as seen in the realm of creative writing and medical diagnostics.

B. Navigating the Ethical Landscape

The case of Tay underlines the non-negotiable imperative to weave ethical considerations into prompt engineering, ensuring that AI behavior adheres to social, cultural, and moral norms.

C. Ensuring Robustness Amidst Complexity

As financial forecasting teaches us, prompts must be deftly engineered to navigate the intricacies and volatilities of complex domains, ensuring that AI outputs are not just accurate but also reliably robust.

Conclusion: The Unfolding Journey of Prompt Engineering

The varied landscapes of successes and failures in real-world applications of prompt engineering offer rich insights, heralding learnings that are crucial in refining our approach towards harnessing AI's generative capabilities. The journey ahead is strewn with unexplored territories and unprecedented challenges. By taking cues from the past and the present, and meticulously crafting our path forward, we steer towards a future where AI not only augments our capabilities but also reflects our ethical, social, and cultural ethos in its interactions and outputs.

Reflective Pause: Engaging with the Unseen

As we step forward, how do we engage with unforeseen challenges in prompt engineering? How do we ensure that as AI systems evolve, our prompt engineering strategies adaptively morph to guide them towards outputs that are accurate, ethical, and contextually relevant?

Through a symbiosis of technological acumen, ethical vigilance, and continuous learning from real-world applications, we embark on an unfolding journey towards mastering the art and science of prompt engineering in the generative AI landscape

8 Future Of Generative AI And Prompt Engineering

Introduction

The future is often a mirror of the past, tempered by current innovations and projected ambitions. As the digital realm blazes ahead, both generative AI and prompt engineering are securing their footholds, with every sign pointing towards them becoming fundamental components of the AI landscape. This chapter delves into the forthcoming trajectories of these two intertwined domains, underpinned by current trends, technological advances, and industry predictions.

Section 1: Emerging Trends in the AI Industry

1. Quantum Computing and AI: Quantum computing, with its parallel processing capabilities, promises to revolutionize AI's computational power. This will lead to AI models that can process complex problems and data sets exponentially faster than current capabilities.

2. Explainable AI (XAI): As AI models become more intricate, there's a mounting need for them to be transparent. XAI aims to make AI decision-making

processes clearer and more understandable, enhancing trust in AI outputs.

3. AI Augmentation: Instead of replacing human tasks, AI is being used to enhance human abilities. Examples include collaborative robots, AI-assisted surgeries, and augmented reality applications guided by AI.

4. Transfer Learning: The ability for AI models to apply knowledge learned in one domain to a different, yet related domain. This minimizes the data required for training in new tasks, making AI models more versatile and efficient.

Section 2: The Evolving Role of Prompt Engineering

1. Customized AI Models: The emphasis will shift from generic AI models to those tailored for specific industries. Prompt engineering will play a pivotal role in customizing these models, ensuring they align with industry-specific nuances and requirements.

2. Dynamic Prompting: Advances in prompt engineering will allow for dynamic and real-time modification of prompts, ensuring AI outputs remain contextually relevant, especially in fast-paced environments like stock trading or emergency response.

3. Human-AI Collaboration: As AI models become more integrated into everyday tasks, prompt engineering will facilitate a more seamless interaction between humans and machines, enhancing collaboration.

4. Automated Prompt Generation: With advancements in AI, there may be an emergence of models that can auto-generate or refine their prompts based on the task's evolving requirements and the feedback received.

Section 3: What to Anticipate in the Next Decade

1. Hyper-personalization: AI will be able to craft deeply personalized experiences for users, from media consumption to shopping. Prompt engineering will ensure that these experiences are not just personalized but are also contextually apt and timely.

2. Ethical AI: As AI becomes more embedded in critical decisions, there'll be a significant push towards ensuring AI behavior is ethically sound. Prompt engineering will be at the forefront of ensuring AI outputs are unbiased and ethical.

3. Integration into Emerging Technologies: Generative AI will find applications in nascent technologies like brain-computer interfaces, advanced robotics, and decentralized web platforms. Prompt engineering will be instrumental in guiding these AIs accurately.

4. Continuous Learning Models: AI models of the future will likely be capable of continuous learning, evolving their knowledge base without the need for periodic retraining. Prompt engineering will adapt to these models, ensuring that prompts remain relevant and effective as the AI learns.

Conclusion

As the horizon of what is technologically feasible continues to expand, generative AI and prompt engineering remain poised to be the torchbearers guiding the AI industry into the future. Their symbiotic relationship ensures that as AI models grow in capability and complexity, there remains a robust mechanism to guide, control, and extract the desired outputs from them. For those keen on remaining at the forefront of AI developments, a keen understanding and continuous adaptation to the trends and advancements in these domains is not just recommended, it's imperative.

Note: As with any predictive content, the trends and anticipations discussed in this chapter are based on current trajectories and may evolve based on unforeseen technological breakthroughs, societal shifts, or global events.

9 Conclusion: Harnessing The Harmonious Dance Of Human Creativity And Generative AI

Conclusion: Harnessing the Harmonious Dance of Human Creativity and Generative AI

Introduction

Our exploration thus far into Generative AI's intricate weavings, from the essence of prompt engineering to ethical considerations and real-world applications, illuminates the vivid tapestry of opportunities and challenges that lie embedded within its folds. In this concluding chapter, we shall reflect upon the symphony of complexities and innovations in the world of generative AI, emphasizing the perennial significance of human creativity and oversight in sculpting its trajectory and applications.

Section 1: The Transformative Arc of Generative AI

1. From Automation to Innovation: Generative AI has transitioned from being a mere tool for automating mundane tasks to becoming a wellspring of innovation, creating content, solutions, and even posing questions that humans might not conceive.

2. Cross-Industry Impact: Sectors ranging from healthcare, finance, and marketing to creative industries like art and writing have witnessed revolutionary changes in operations, customer engagement, and problem-solving, emanating from the effective utilization of generative AI.

3. Enhanced Decision-Making: In the decision-making crucibles of businesses and governance, generative AI provides enriched data analysis, foresight, and problem-solving capabilities, thereby shaping informed, data-driven decisions.

Section 2: The Intrinsic Role of Human Creativity

1. Guiding the AI Muse: While generative AI can concoct a plethora of creative outputs, it is the human creativity that gives it direction, intent, and purpose, ensuring

that the AI's creations are not just innovative but also meaningful and contextually relevant.

2. Ethical and Moral Stewardship: Human oversight safeguards the moral and ethical deployment of AI, ensuring that its applications and creations adhere to our societal norms, values, and legislative frameworks.

3. Symbiotic Creativity: The amalgamation of human ingenuity and AI's computational prowess paves the way for a new epoch of creativity, where artists, writers, and creators leverage AI's capabilities to explore uncharted territories of innovation.

Section 3: The Interplay of Human and AI Creativity

1. Complementary Capacities: The juxtaposition of human emotional intelligence with AI's data-driven objectivity provides a balanced, rich substrate for unbridled creative and innovative endeavors.

2. Collaborative Exploration: Engaging in a collaborative discourse with AI, humans can explore novel ideas, challenge existing paradigms, and weave a future tapestry that is both technologically advanced and humanely sensitive.

3. Learning and Evolution: The iterative cycle of learning between human feedback and AI output evolution signifies a path towards refined, efficient, and impactful AI applications across the board.

Section 4: Toward a Future Etched by Co-creation

1. Inclusive Future: A future where generative AI is not a mere tool but a co-creator, working in tandem with human creators, ensuring that technological advancements and creative explorations are mutually inclusive and universally accessible.

2. Redefining Creativity: The convergence of human and AI creativity will redefine creative processes, methodologies, and even our perception of what constitutes creativity in the digital age.

3. Navigating Uncharted Terrains: Together, human and AI will explore and navigate through unknown realms of possibilities, crafting a future that harmoniously blends technological prowess with human emotional and creative depth.

Closing Reflection

The canvas of the future, splashed with the vibrant colors of generative AI and the subtle, intricate strokes of human creativity, is not merely a depiction of coexistence but a vibrant portrayal of co-creation. It is imperative to realize that the technological marvel of generative AI is not here to supersede human capabilities but to augment them, opening new horizons for exploration, innovation, and creation. As we step into the future, let us embrace the symbiotic relationship that intertwines human creativity with AI's capabilities, crafting a future narrative that is not just technologically advanced but also ethically sound, creatively rich, and fundamentally human.

Note: The insights, perspectives, and anticipations presented herein are rooted in current technological, societal, and industry contexts and are subject to evolution with the unfolding tapestry of technological advancements, policy formulations, and societal shifts.

10 1000+ GPT-4 AI Prompts

Email Marketing Prompts

1. "I need a [type of email] that will make my [ideal customer persona] feel [emotion] about my [product/service] and persuade them to take [desired action] with a sense of urgency."
2. "I'm looking for a [type of email] that will speak directly to the needs and pain points of my [ideal customer persona] and persuade them to take [desired action] with a sense of urgency and strong offer."
3. "I need a [type of email] that will showcase the value and benefits of my [product/service] to [ideal customer persona] and convince them to take [desired action] with social proof and credibility building elements."
4. "I'm looking for a [type of email] that will clearly explain the features and benefits of my [product/service] to [ideal customer persona] and persuade them to make a purchase with a strong call-to-action."
5. "I need a [type of email] that will convince my [ideal customer persona] to purchase my [product/service] by

highlighting its unique benefits and addressing any potential objections."

6. "I'm looking for a [type of email] that will establish trust and credibility with my [ideal customer persona] by highlighting the successes and testimonials of previous customers who have used my [product/service]."

7. "I need a [type of email] that will overcome objections and concerns my [ideal customer persona] may have about my [product/service] and convince them to take [desired action]."

8. "I'm looking for a [type of email] that will showcase the unique features and benefits of my [product/service] to [ideal customer persona] and persuade them to make a purchase."

9. "I need a [type of email] that will tell a story about my [product/service] and how it has helped [ideal customer persona] achieve their [goal] in a relatable and engaging way."

10. "I'm looking for a [type of email] that will draw in my [ideal customer persona] with a strong headline and hook, and then convince them to take [desired action] with persuasive language and compelling evidence."

11. "I'm looking for a [type of email] that will explain the features and benefits of my [product/service] to [ideal

customer persona] in a clear and concise manner, leading them to make a purchase."
12. "I need a [type of email] that will make my [ideal customer persona] feel [emotion] about my [product/service] and convince them to take [desired action]."
13. "I need a [type of email] that will persuade my [ideal customer persona] to purchase my [product/service] by highlighting its unique benefits and addressing any potential objections."
14. "I'm looking for a [type of email] that will convince my [ideal customer persona] to sign up for my [program/subscription] by explaining the value it brings and the benefits they'll receive."
15. "I need a [type of email] that will address the pain points and needs of my [ideal customer persona] and show them how my [product/service] is the solution they've been searching for."

Copywriting Prompts

1. "Please write a compelling [type of text] that speaks directly to my [ideal customer persona] and encourages them to take [desired action] on my [website/product]."

Generative AI: Unleashing Creative Genius with Prompt Engineering

2. "I need a [type of text] that will persuade [ideal customer persona] to purchase my [product/service] by highlighting its unique benefits and addressing any potential objections."

3. "I'm looking for a [type of text] that will convince [ideal customer persona] to sign up for my [program/subscription] by explaining the value it brings and the benefits they'll receive."

4. "I need a [type of text] that will make my [ideal customer persona] feel [emotion] about my [product/service] and convince them to take [desired action]."

5. "I'm looking for a [type of text] that will explain the features and benefits of my [product/service] to [ideal customer persona] in a clear and concise manner, leading them to make a purchase."

6. "I need a [type of text] that will address the pain points and needs of my [ideal customer persona] and show them how my [product/service] is the solution they've been searching for."

7. "I'm looking for a [type of text] that will draw in my [ideal customer persona] with a strong headline and hook, and then convince them to take [desired action] with persuasive language and compelling evidence."

8. "I need a [type of text] that will tell a story about my [product/service] and how it has helped [ideal customer

persona] achieve their [goal] in a relatable and engaging way."

9. "I'm looking for a [type of text] that will showcase the unique features and benefits of my [product/service] to [ideal customer persona] and persuade them to make a purchase."

10. "I need a [type of text] that will overcome objections and concerns my [ideal customer persona] may have about my [product/service] and convince them to take [desired action]."

11. "I'm looking for a [type of text] that will establish trust and credibility with my [ideal customer persona] by highlighting the successes and testimonials of previous customers who have used my [product/service]."

12. "I need a [type of text] that will make my [ideal customer persona] feel [emotion] about my [product/service] and persuade them to take [desired action] with a sense of urgency."

13. "I'm looking for a [type of text] that will clearly explain the features and benefits of my [product/service] to [ideal customer persona] and persuade them to make a purchase with a strong call-to-action."

14. "I need a [type of text] that will showcase the value and benefits of my [product/service] to [ideal customer

persona] and convince them to take [desired action] with social proof and credibility-building elements."
15. "I'm looking for a [type of text] that will speak directly to the needs and pain points of my [ideal customer persona] and persuade them to take [desired action] with a sense of urgency and strong offer."
16. What is the purpose of a copywriting strategy, and why is it important for businesses to have one?
17. What are the key components of a copywriting strategy, and how do they work together to create effective copy?
18. How do you conduct research and analysis to inform your copywriting strategy, and what factors should you consider?
19. What are the characteristics of an ideal target audience, and how do you identify and understand them in the context of copywriting?
20. How do you define your unique selling proposition (USP) and incorporate it into your copywriting strategy?
21. What are the different stages of the customer journey, and how can you tailor your copywriting strategy to address each stage effectively?
22. How do you create buyer personas to inform your copywriting strategy, and what information should you include in them?

23. How do you differentiate your product or service from competitors in your copywriting, and what techniques can you use to do so?
24. How do you use emotional appeals in your copywriting strategy to connect with readers and drive conversions?
25. What are the key principles of effective storytelling in copywriting, and how can they be applied to various industries and niches?
26. How do you craft headlines and subject lines that grab attention and entice readers to keep reading?
27. What are some techniques for structuring copy in a way that is easy to read and visually appealing, such as using headings, subheadings, and bullet points?
28. How do you use customer testimonials and social proof to build credibility and trust in your copywriting?
29. What role does formatting play in copywriting, and what are some best practices for using typography, color, and images effectively?
30. How do you optimize copy for search engines without sacrificing readability and persuasiveness?
31. What are some common mistakes to avoid in copywriting, such as using jargon, being too salesy, or failing to proofread?

32. How do you ensure that your copywriting reflects your brand voice and values, and is consistent across all channels and platforms?
33. How do you set and measure goals for your copywriting, and what metrics should you track to evaluate success?
34. What are some tips for writing compelling calls-to-action (CTAs) that encourage readers to take action?
35. How can you use data and analytics to optimize your copywriting and improve results over time?
36. What are some best practices for crafting effective email copy, such as subject lines, preheaders, and body content?
37. How do you tailor your copywriting to different stages of the sales funnel, such as awareness, consideration, and decision?
38. How do you adapt your copywriting strategy for different audiences, such as B2B, B2C, or niche markets?
39. How do you incorporate keywords and phrases into your copywriting to improve search engine rankings and visibility?
40. What are some strategies for creating content that is shareable and has the potential to go viral?
41. What are some common mistakes that copywriters make when crafting headlines and subject lines, and how can they be avoided?

42. What role do emotions and psychology play in writing effective headlines and subject lines?
43. How important is it to use keywords in headlines and subject lines, and what are some best practices for doing so without sacrificing clarity or creativity?
44. What are some effective strategies for writing attention-grabbing headlines and subject lines that are relevant to the content of the piece?
45. How can copywriters use humor and wordplay to make headlines and subject lines more memorable and engaging?
46. How can copywriters tailor their headlines and subject lines to different channels and platforms, such as social media, email marketing, and search engine results pages?
47. What are some best practices for writing headlines and subject lines that are SEO-friendly without sacrificing readability or creativity?
48. How can copywriters use statistics and numbers to make headlines and subject lines more compelling and credible?
49. What are some effective strategies for using questions in headlines and subject lines to engage readers and pique their curiosity?

50. How can copywriters use sensory words and vivid imagery to make headlines and subject lines more appealing to readers?
51. What role do formatting and typography play in creating effective headlines and subject lines, and what are some best practices for using these elements to your advantage?
52. How important is it to test different headlines and subject lines to see what works best, and what are some best practices for doing so?
53. How can copywriters use personalization and segmentation to make headlines and subject lines more relevant and engaging to specific audiences?
54. How can copywriters use storytelling and narrative techniques in their headlines and subject lines to create a sense of intrigue and emotional connection with readers?
55. What are some effective strategies for using urgency and scarcity in headlines and subject lines to motivate readers to take action?
56. How can copywriters use cultural references and trends to make headlines and subject lines more relatable and shareable?

57. What are some best practices for writing headlines and subject lines that are concise and to-the-point, while still being compelling and engaging?
58. How can copywriters use social proof and testimonials in headlines and subject lines to build credibility and trust with readers?
59. How important is it to create a sense of exclusivity or insider knowledge in headlines and subject lines, and what are some effective strategies for doing so?
60. What are some effective strategies for using contrast and comparison in headlines and subject lines to highlight the benefits of a product or service?
61. How can copywriters use power words and action verbs to create a sense of urgency and excitement in headlines and subject lines?
62. What role do cultural and societal trends play in creating effective headlines and subject lines, and how can copywriters leverage these trends to their advantage?
63. How can copywriters use shock value or controversy in headlines and subject lines to grab readers' attention, while still being ethical and responsible?
64. What are some best practices for writing headlines and subject lines that are inclusive and avoid stereotypes or offensive language?

65. How can copywriters use A/B testing and other analytics to continuously refine and optimize their headlines and subject lines over time?
66. What are some common misconceptions that beginner copywriters have about the profession, and how can they be corrected?
67. How important is research in the copywriting process, and what are some tips for conducting effective research?
68. What are some common mistakes that beginner copywriters make in understanding their target audience, and how can these mistakes be avoided?
69. How do you avoid writing copy that is too salesy or pushy, and instead create copy that is engaging and persuasive?
70. How do you write headlines that grab the reader's attention and encourage them to keep reading?
71. What are some common grammar and punctuation mistakes that beginner copywriters make, and how can they be avoided?
72. How do you avoid using jargon or technical language that can be confusing or alienating to the reader?
73. What are some tips for writing copy that is easy to read and understand, such as using short sentences and paragraphs?

74. How do you avoid using clichés or overused phrases that can make copywriting seem boring or unoriginal?
75. What are some tips for using humor or other forms of entertainment in copywriting, and how can these be done effectively?
76. How do you avoid making assumptions about the reader's preferences or experiences, and instead write copy that is relevant and relatable?
77. What are some common mistakes that beginner copywriters make in creating calls to action, and how can these be avoided?
78. How do you avoid creating copy that is too similar to the competition, and instead create copy that is unique and memorable?
79. What are some tips for writing copy that is SEO-friendly, such as using keywords and meta descriptions?
80. How do you avoid using hyperbole or making promises that cannot be kept in your copywriting?
81. What are some common mistakes that beginner copywriters make in structuring their copy, and how can they be avoided?
82. How do you avoid writing copy that is too long or wordy, and instead create copy that is concise and impactful?
83. What are some tips for writing copy that is authentic and genuine, and avoids sounding insincere or fake?

84. How do you avoid using too many adjectives or adverbs, and instead write copy that is simple and direct?
85. What are some common mistakes that beginner copywriters make in proofreading and editing, and how can these be avoided?
86. How do you avoid creating copy that is too generic or broad, and instead create copy that is targeted and specific?
87. What are some tips for writing copy that is appropriate for different channels, such as social media, email, or print ads?
88. How do you avoid creating copy that is too complicated or technical, and instead create copy that is accessible and easy to understand?
89. What are some common mistakes that beginner copywriters make in understanding the client's goals and objectives, and how can these be avoided?
90. How do you avoid getting discouraged or overwhelmed when starting out in copywriting, and instead maintain motivation and focus?
91. What are some key elements that make copy compelling, and how can copywriters incorporate them into their writing?

92. How important is understanding the target audience in creating compelling copy, and what are some tips for doing so effectively?
93. What are some strategies for writing headlines that grab the reader's attention and draw them into the copy?
94. How can copywriters use storytelling to create more engaging and compelling copy?
95. How do you avoid writing copy that is too salesy or pushy, and instead create copy that is persuasive and engaging?
96. What are some tips for writing copy that is clear and easy to understand, even for complex products or services?
97. How can copywriters use emotional appeals to create more compelling copy, and what are some best practices for doing so?
98. How important is creating a strong value proposition in creating compelling copy, and how can this be done effectively?
99. What are some common mistakes that copywriters make in trying to write compelling copy, and how can these be avoided?
100. How can copywriters use data and statistics to create more persuasive and compelling copy?

101. What are some strategies for using humor or other forms of entertainment in copywriting, and how can these be done effectively?
102. How can copywriters use customer testimonials or social proof to create more compelling copy?
103. How important is creating a sense of urgency or scarcity in creating compelling copy, and what are some ways to do so effectively?
104. How can copywriters use visual elements, such as images or videos, to create more engaging and compelling copy?
105. What are some tips for writing copy that is tailored to specific channels, such as social media or email marketing?
106. How can copywriters use tone and voice to create more compelling copy, and what are some best practices for doing so?
107. What are some common mistakes that copywriters make in using language that is too complex or technical, and how can these be avoided?
108. How can copywriters use sensory language to create more engaging and compelling copy?
109. How important is creating a strong call-to-action in creating compelling copy, and what are some best practices for doing so?

110. How can copywriters use personalization to create more compelling copy, and what are some best practices for doing so?
111. How can copywriters use the power of association to create more persuasive and compelling copy?
112. What are some tips for creating copy that is memorable and stands out from the competition?
113. How can copywriters use the power of persuasion to create more compelling copy, and what are some best practices for doing so?
114. How can copywriters use current events or trending topics to create more engaging and compelling copy?
115. How important is testing and optimization in creating compelling copy, and what are some strategies for doing so effectively?
116. What are some resources you rely on to stay informed about the latest copywriting trends and techniques?
117. How often do you seek out new information on copywriting, and how do you prioritize what to learn next?
118. What are some of the biggest changes you've seen in copywriting over the last few years, and how have you adapted to them?

119. How important is it to stay on top of emerging technologies, and how do you incorporate new tech trends into your work?
120. What are some online communities or groups you participate in to stay informed about the latest copywriting trends and techniques?
121. How do you track your progress in learning new copywriting skills and techniques, and what metrics do you use to measure your success?
122. What are some of the most common mistakes that copywriters make when trying to stay up-to-date with new trends and techniques?
123. How do you balance the need to stay current with the desire to maintain a unique voice and style in your copywriting?
124. How do you incorporate feedback and criticism from others when learning and experimenting with new copywriting techniques?
125. How important is it to experiment with new techniques and strategies in your copywriting, and what are some best practices for doing so?
126. What role do you think creativity and innovation play in copywriting, and how do you foster those qualities in your work?

127. How do you adapt to changes in the target audience's preferences and behaviors, and how does this affect your copywriting strategies?
128. What are some ways to stay on top of emerging social media and digital marketing trends, and how do you incorporate them into your copywriting strategies?
129. How important is collaboration with other professionals, such as designers and marketers, in staying current with the latest copywriting trends and techniques?
130. How do you balance the need for consistency in your copywriting with the desire to try new things and stay on top of emerging trends?
131. What are some of the most significant challenges you've faced in staying up-to-date with new copywriting trends and techniques, and how have you overcome them?
132. How do you identify emerging trends and techniques that are worth investing time and resources in learning, versus those that are more passing fads?
133. What are some best practices for staying organized and managing your time effectively when trying to learn new copywriting skills and techniques?
134. How do you leverage industry events and conferences to stay informed about the latest copywriting trends and techniques?

135. What are some ways to stay motivated and engaged when learning new copywriting skills and techniques?
136. How do you balance the need for continuous learning and growth with the need to focus on producing high-quality work for clients?
137. What are some tools and resources you use to stay on top of the latest trends in SEO and other key digital marketing strategies?
138. How do you incorporate user experience (UX) design principles into your copywriting, and what are some best practices for doing so?
139. What are some ways to stay informed about emerging trends in content marketing, and how do you incorporate them into your copywriting strategies?
140. How do you balance the need to stay informed about emerging trends with the need to maintain a focus on the core principles of effective copywriting, such as clarity and persuasive messaging?
141. What is the role of storytelling in copywriting, and why is it important for businesses to incorporate it into their marketing strategy?
142. How can storytelling be used to create an emotional connection between a brand and its customers?
143. What are some common types of brand stories, such as origin stories, customer success stories, or employee

stories, and how can they be used effectively in copywriting?

144. How do you identify and define the key elements of a brand story, such as the protagonist, the conflict, and the resolution?

145. How do you tailor your brand story to different audiences, such as potential customers, investors, or employees?

146. What are some effective techniques for using descriptive language and sensory details to make a brand story more vivid and engaging?

147. How do you create a brand story that is both authentic and compelling, and avoids cliches or stereotypes?

148. What are some examples of brands that use storytelling effectively in their copywriting, and what can we learn from their success?

149. How do you use storytelling to differentiate a brand from its competitors, and create a unique value proposition?

150. What are some tips for incorporating storytelling into different types of copywriting, such as social media posts, blog articles, or email newsletters?

151. How do you measure the effectiveness of storytelling in copywriting, and what metrics should you track to evaluate success?

152. How can businesses use user-generated content or customer stories in their copywriting to build a sense of community and social proof?
153. How do you use humor, irony, or other literary devices in your brand storytelling to create a memorable and distinctive voice?
154. How do you use storytelling to address social or environmental issues, and position your brand as socially responsible or ethical?
155. How do you create a narrative arc in your brand story, and use it to guide the reader's journey and emotional response?
156. What are some common mistakes to avoid in using storytelling in copywriting, such as being too self-promotional or ignoring the audience's needs?
157. How do you use data and analytics to refine your brand story, and adjust it to changing market conditions or customer preferences?
158. How do you use storytelling to build a consistent and coherent brand narrative across all channels and touchpoints?
159. What are some ethical considerations in using storytelling in copywriting, such as avoiding stereotypes or misrepresentations?

160. How do you use storytelling to create a sense of urgency or immediacy in your copywriting, and motivate readers to take action?
161. How can businesses use personal anecdotes in their copywriting to create a relatable brand story that resonates with customers?
162. How can businesses use the hero's journey narrative structure in their copywriting to create a compelling brand story?
163. Can you give me examples of how businesses have successfully used customer stories in their copywriting to build a strong brand narrative?
164. How can businesses use the power of metaphors and analogies in their copywriting to help customers understand complex ideas and connect with the brand on a deeper level?
165. How can businesses use emotional storytelling in their copywriting to create a more powerful connection with customers and build a strong brand identity?

YouTube Ad Scripts Prompts

1. "I need a YouTube ad script that will provide valuable and relevant information to my [ideal customer persona] and persuade them to take [desired action] on my [website/product]."

2. "I need a YouTube ad script that will showcase the unique features and benefits of my [product/service] to my [ideal customer persona] and persuade them to make a purchase with social proof and credibility-building elements."

3. "I need a YouTube ad script that will overcome objections and concerns my [ideal customer persona] may have about my [product/service] and convince them to take [desired action] with a sense of urgency."

4. "I'm looking for a YouTube ad script that will introduce my [product/service] to my [ideal customer persona] and persuade them to take [desired action] with a strong call-to-action and compelling visuals."

5. "I'm looking for a YouTube ad script that will showcase the value and benefits of my [product/service] to my [ideal customer persona] and persuade them to take [desired action] with a strong offer and clear call-to-action."

6. "I'm looking for a YouTube ad script that will clearly explain the features and benefits of my [product/service] to my [ideal customer persona] and persuade them to make a purchase with a sense of urgency."

7. "I need a YouTube ad script that will tell a story about my [product/service] and how it has helped [ideal customer

persona] achieve their [goal] in a relatable and engaging way."

8. "I'm looking for a YouTube ad script that will draw in my [ideal customer persona] with a strong headline and hook, and then convince them to take [desired action] with persuasive language and compelling evidence."

9. "I'm looking for a YouTube ad script that will speak directly to the needs and pain points of my [ideal customer persona] and persuade them to take [desired action] with a sense of urgency and strong offer."

10. "I need a YouTube ad script that will address the pain points and needs of my [ideal customer persona] and show them how my [product/service] is the solution they've been searching for."

11. "I'm looking for a YouTube ad script that will establish trust and credibility with my [ideal customer persona] by highlighting the successes and testimonials of previous customers who have used my [product/service]."

12. "I need a YouTube ad script that will educate my [ideal customer persona] on a specific [topic] and persuade them to take [desired action] on my [website/product]."

13. "I need a YouTube ad script that will showcase the unique selling points of my [product/service] and persuade my [ideal customer persona] to make a purchase with a sense of urgency and exclusive offers."

14. "I'm looking for a YouTube ad script that will draw in my [ideal customer persona] with a relatable and authentic message, and then persuade them to take [desired action] with a strong call-to action and compelling visuals."
15. "I'm looking for a YouTube ad script that will engage my [ideal customer persona] with a unique and compelling perspective on [subject] and persuade them to take [desired action] on my [website/product]."

Facebook Ad Copy Prompts

1. "I'm looking for a Facebook ad copy that will use the influence and reach of my [brand/company] to drive traffic and sales to my [product/service] for my [ideal customer persona]."
2. "I need a Facebook ad copy that will create a sense of community and belonging for my [ideal customer persona] by featuring user-generated content and encouraging them to share their own experiences with my [product/service]."
3. "I'm looking for a Facebook ad copy that will provide a sneak peek of upcoming products or services and create a sense of anticipation and excitement for my [ideal

customer persona] with a clear and compelling call-to-action."

4. "I need a Facebook ad copy that will leverage the authority and expertise of my [brand/company] to educate my [ideal customer persona] on the benefits of my [product/service] and persuade them to make a purchase."

5. "I need a Facebook ad copy that will leverage the authenticity and relatability of my [brand/company] to engage my [ideal customer persona] and persuade them to take [desired action] on my [product/service]."

6. "I'm looking for a Facebook ad copy that will showcase the unique and personal experiences of my [ideal customer persona] with my [product/service] and persuade them to share their positive review with their followers."

7. "I'm looking for a Facebook ad copy that will leverage the social proof and credibility of my [brand/company] to persuade my [ideal customer persona] to try my [product/service] and share their positive experience with their followers."

8. "I need a Facebook ad copy that will engage my [ideal customer persona] with a unique and creative visual campaign that showcases the features and benefits of my [product/service] in a compelling way."

9. "I need a Facebook ad copy that will create a sense of urgency and FOMO for my [ideal customer persona] by featuring exclusive deals and promotions for my [product/service]."
10. "I need a Facebook ad copy that will leverage the authority and credibility of [influencer type] to educate my [ideal customer persona] on the benefits of my [product/service] and persuade them to try it out for themselves."
11. "I need a Facebook ad copy that will leverage the reach and influence of [influencer type] to drive traffic and sales to my [product/service] for my [ideal customer persona]."
12. "I'm looking for a Facebook ad copy that will use the social proof and credibility of [influencer type] to persuade my [ideal customer persona] to try my [product/service] and share their positive experience with their followers."
13. "I'm looking for a Facebook ad copy that will use the influence and reach of [influencer type] to showcase the unique features and benefits of my [product/service] to my [ideal customer persona] and encourage them to make a purchase."
14. "I need a Facebook ad copy that will engage my [ideal customer persona] with [specific type of content] from

[influencer type] who can authentically share the benefits of my [product/service] and encourage them to make a purchase."

15. "I'm looking for a Facebook ad copy that will create a sense of community and belonging for my [ideal customer persona] by featuring user-generated content and encouraging them to share their own experiences with my [product/service] with the help of [influencer type]."

Twitter Thread Ideas Prompts

1. "I'm looking for a Twitter thread idea that will provide valuable and relevant information to my [ideal customer persona] about [subject] and attract high-quality leads with a strong call-to action."
2. "I'm looking for a Twitter thread idea that will tell a unique and relatable story about my [product/service] and how it has helped [ideal customer persona] achieve their [goal]."
3. "I need a Twitter thread idea that will showcase the unique features and benefits of my [product/service] in a fun and creative way, and attract high-quality leads with a strong offer."

Generative AI: Unleashing Creative Genius with Prompt Engineering

4. "I need a Twitter thread idea that will both go viral and attract high-quality leads for my [product/service] with a strong call-to-action and compelling visuals."
5. "I'm looking for a Twitter thread idea that will showcase the value and benefits of my [product/service] to my [ideal customer persona] and persuade them to take [desired action] with a clear and compelling message."
6. "I need a Twitter thread idea that will overcome objections and concerns my [ideal customer persona] may have about my [product/service] and convince them to take [desired action] with a sense of urgency."
7. "I need a Twitter thread idea that will engage my [ideal customer persona] with a unique and compelling perspective on [subject] and persuade them to take [desired action] on my [website/product]."
8. "I'm looking for a Twitter thread idea that will go viral and showcase my [product/service] to my [ideal customer persona] in a creative and engaging way."
9. "I'm looking for a Twitter thread idea that will establish trust and credibility with my [ideal customer persona] by showcasing the success stories of previous customers who have used my [product/service]."
10. "I'm looking for a Twitter thread idea that will compare my [product/service] to similar options on the market

and persuade my [ideal customer persona] to choose us with clear and compelling evidence."

11. "I'm looking for a Twitter thread idea that will provide a behind-the-scenes look at my [company/brand] and persuade my [ideal customer persona] to take [desired action] with a sense of authenticity and relatability."

12. "I need a Twitter thread idea that will showcase the unique selling points of my [product/service] and attract high-quality leads with a sense of urgency and exclusive offers."

13. "I need a Twitter thread idea that will provide a step-by-step guide on how to use my [product/service] and attract high-quality leads with clear and compelling instructions."

14. "I need a Twitter thread idea that will draw in my [ideal customer persona] with a relatable and authentic message, and then persuade them to take [desired action] with a strong call-to-action and compelling visuals."

15. What are some common misconceptions about [topic]?
16. How has [topic] evolved?
17. What are some key benefits of [product/service]?wh
18. How can [product/service] be used in everyday life?
19. What are some tips for improving [skill]?
20. What are some common mistakes to avoid when [task]?

21. What are some notable examples of [concept] in action?
22. What are some emerging trends in [industry]?
23. How has [industry] been impacted by recent events?
24. What are some challenges facing [industry]?
25. What are some ethical considerations related to [topic]?
26. How can [topic] be made more inclusive?
27. What are some common myths about [topic]?
28. What are some frequently asked questions about [topic]?
29. What are some surprising facts about [topic]?
30. What are some common myths about [product/service]?
31. How has [topic] been portrayed in popular culture?
32. What are some notable individuals who have contributed to [topic]?
33. How can [product/service] be used to improve [aspect] of life?
34. What are some alternative approaches to [task]?
35. What are some potential benefits of [concept]?
36. What are some potential drawbacks of [concept]?
37. What are some successful case studies of [topic]?
38. What are some common misconceptions about [industry]?
39. What are some successful examples of [product/service] in use?
40. What are some common challenges facing [industry] professionals?

41. What are some best practices for [task]?
42. What are some potential future developments in [industry]?
43. What are some notable achievements related to [topic]?
44. What are some key differences between [product/service] and its competitors?
45. How has [product/service] been received by consumers?
46. What are some common pitfalls to avoid when [task]?
47. What are some common challenges facing [industry] professionals?
48. What are some notable achievements related to [topic]?
49. What are some key differences between [product/service] and its competitors?
50. How has [product/service] been received by consumers?
51. What are some common pitfalls to avoid when [task]?
52. What are some potential benefits of [concept]?
53. What are some potential drawbacks of [concept]?
54. How can [topic] be used to promote social change?
55. How has [industry] been impacted by advances in technology?
56. What are some notable inventions related to [topic]?
57. What are some emerging markets in [industry]?
58. How has [topic] impacted society as a whole?
59. How can [product/service] be adapted to meet changing consumer needs?

60. What are some common challenges facing [industry] professionals?
61. How can [product/service] be used to solve common problems?
62. What are some notable case studies related to [topic]?
63. What are some emerging trends in [industry]?
64. What are some potential future developments in [industry]?
65. What are some common misconceptions about [product/service]?
66. How can [product/service] be made more accessible?
67. How has [topic] been impacted by changes in legislation?
68. What are some successful examples of [concept] in practice?
69. What are some notable individuals who have contributed to [industry]?
70. How can [product/service] be used to promote sustainability?
71. What are some emerging technologies in [industry]?
72. What are some key challenges facing [industry] in the coming years?
73. What are some common myths about [industry]?
74. How can [topic] be used to drive innovation?
75. What are some best practices for [industry] professionals?

76. What are some notable milestones in the history of [topic]?
77. How can [product/service] be customized to meet individual needs?
78. What are some common misconceptions about [topic] in the media?
79. What are some successful examples of [product/service] in the global market?
80. How can [product/service] be adapted to meet cultural differences?
81. What are some ethical dilemmas faced by [industry] professionals?
82. How has [industry] been impacted by globalization?
83. What are some notable individuals who have contributed to the advancement of [topic]?
84. What are some potential risks associated with [concept]?
85. How can [product/service] be used to enhance productivity?
86. What are some common trends in [industry] that are driving innovation?
87. What are some notable examples of [industry] collaboration?
88. How can [product/service] be used to improve accessibility for people with disabilities?
89. What are some emerging business models in [industry]?

90. What are some successful examples of companies implementing [topic] into their strategy?
91. How has [industry] been impacted by changing consumer behavior?
92. What are some common challenges faced by startups in [industry]?
93. What are some notable examples of companies making strides towards sustainability in [industry]?
94. How can [product/service] be used to drive social impact?
95. What are some emerging trends in marketing [product/service]?
96. What are some best practices for building [product/service] brand awareness?
97. How has [topic] impacted the lives of individuals in different communities?
98. What are some successful examples of [industry] companies collaborating with non-profit organizations?
99. What are some common mistakes made by businesses when introducing [product/service] to the market?
100. How has [product/service] impacted the economy?

Generative AI: Unleashing Creative Genius with Prompt Engineering

YouTube Video Ideas Prompts

1. "I need a YouTube video idea that will both go viral and persuade my [ideal customer persona] to take [desired action] on my [website/product] with a strong call-to-action and compelling visuals."
2. "I'm looking for a YouTube video idea that will tell a unique and relatable story about my [product/service] and how it has helped [ideal customer persona] achieve their [goal]."
3. "I need a YouTube video idea that will showcase the unique features and benefits of my [product/service] in a fun and creative way, and persuade my [ideal customer persona] to make a purchase."
4. "I'm looking for a YouTube video idea that will showcase the value and benefits of my [product/service] to my [ideal customer persona] and persuade them to take [desired action] with a strong offer and clear call-to-action."
5. "I'm looking for a YouTube video idea that will provide valuable and relevant information to my [ideal customer persona] about [subject] and persuade them to take [desired action] on my [website/product]."
6. "I need a YouTube video idea that will overcome objections and concerns my [ideal customer persona]

may have about my [product/service] and convince them to take [desired action] with a sense of urgency."

7. "I'm looking for a YouTube video idea that will go viral and showcase my [product/service] to my [ideal customer persona] in a creative and entertaining way."

8. "I need a YouTube video idea that will showcase the success stories of previous customers who have used my [product/service] and persuade my [ideal customer persona] to make a purchase."

9. "I need a YouTube video idea that will engage my [ideal customer persona] with a unique and compelling perspective on [subject] and persuade them to take [desired action] on my [website/product]."

10. "I need a YouTube video idea that will provide a behind-the-scenes look at my [company/brand] and persuade my [ideal customer persona] to take [desired action] with a sense of authenticity and relatability."

11. "I'm looking for a YouTube video idea that will provide a step-by-step guide on how to use my [product/service] and persuade my [ideal customer persona] to make a purchase with clear and compelling instructions."

12. "I'm looking for a YouTube video idea that will draw in my [ideal customer persona] with a relatable and authentic message, and then persuade them to take

[desired action] with a strong call-to-action and compelling visuals."

13. "I'm looking for a YouTube video idea that will showcase the unique selling points of my [product/service] and persuade my [ideal customer persona] to make a purchase with a sense of urgency and exclusive offers."

14. "I need a YouTube video idea that will demonstrate how my [product/service] can solve the specific pain points and needs of my [ideal customer persona] in a relatable and engaging way."

15. "I need a YouTube video idea that will compare my [product/service] to similar options on the market and persuade my [ideal customer persona] to choose us with clear and compelling evidence.

ChatGPT SEO Prompts

1. "I'm looking for ways to optimize my website's title tags and meta descriptions for on-page SEO for my website about '{topic}'."
2. "I'm looking for ways to improve my website's load time and page speed for on-page SEO for my website about '{topic}'."
3. "I'm looking for ways to create and optimize my website's content for on-page SEO for my website about '{topic}'."

4. "I'm looking for ways to use header tags and structure my website's content for on-page SEO for my website about '{topic}'."
5. "I'm looking for ways to optimize my website's images and videos for on-page SEO for my website about '{topic}'."
6. "I'm looking for ways to use internal linking for on-page SEO for my website about '{topic}'."
7. "I'm looking for ways to use alt tags for images for on-page SEO for my website about '{topic}'."
8. "I'm looking for ways to use schema markup for on-page SEO for my website about '{topic}'."
9. "I'm looking for ways to use keyword research and targeting for on-page SEO for my website about '{topic}'."
10. "I'm looking for ways to improve my website's on-page SEO through the use of structured data for '{topic}'."
11. "I'm looking for ways to improve my website's accessibility for on-page SEO for my website about '{topic}'"
12. "I'm looking for ways to use social media tags for on-page SEO for my website about '{topic}'"
13. "I'm looking for ways to improve my website's mobile optimization for on-page SEO for my website about '{topic}'"

14. "I'm looking for ways to use redirects and 404 error pages for on-page SEO for my website about '{topic}'"
15. "I'm looking for ways to use analytics and tracking for on-page SEO for my website about '{topic}'"
16. "I'm looking for ways to use structured data markup for on-page SEO for my website about '{topic}'"
17. "I'm looking for ways to use canonical tags for on-page SEO for my website about '{topic}'"
18. "I'm looking for ways to improve my website's URL structure for on-page SEO for my website about '{topic}'"
19. "I'm looking for ways to use rich snippets for on-page SEO for my website about '{topic}'"
20. "I'm looking for ways to improve my website's on-page SEO by creating a sitemap for '{topic}'"
21. "I'm looking for ways to improve my website's on-page SEO by optimizing my website's HTML code for '{topic}'"
22. "I'm looking for ways to use meta robots tags for on-page SEO for my website about '{topic}'"
23. "I'm looking for ways to improve my website's on-page SEO by creating a robots.txt file for '{topic}'"
24. "I'm looking for ways to optimize my website's on-page SEO by using schema.org for '{topic}'"
25. "I'm looking for ways to improve my website's on-page SEO by using JSON-LD for '{topic}'"

26. "I'm looking for ways to use breadcrumb navigation for on-page SEO for my website about '{topic}'"
27. "I'm looking for ways to use rich media for on-page SEO for my website about '{topic}'"
28. "I'm looking for ways to use multimedia for on-page SEO for my website about '{topic}'"
29. "I'm looking for ways to improve my website's on-page SEO by using internal linking and anchor texts for '{topic}'"
30. "I'm looking for ways to improve my website's on-page SEO by optimizing my website's XML sitemap for '{topic}'"

Cold DM Ideas Prompts

1. "I'm looking for a cold DM idea that will use the influence and reach of my [brand/company] to drive traffic and sales to my [product/service] for my [ideal customer persona]."
2. "I need a cold DM idea that will provide valuable and relevant information to my [ideal customer persona] about [subject] and persuade them to take [desired action] with a personalized message."
3. "I need a cold DM idea that will draw in my [ideal customer persona] with a relatable and authentic message, and then persuade them to take [desired

action] with a strong call-to-action and compelling visuals."

4. "I'm looking for a cold DM idea that will showcase the unique features and benefits of my [product/service] to my [ideal customer persona] in a clear and compelling way."

5. "I'm looking for a cold DM idea that will provide a step-by-step guide on how to use my [product/service] and persuade my [ideal customer persona] to make a purchase with clear and compelling instructions."

6. "I need a cold DM idea that will showcase the success stories of previous customers who have used my [product/service] and persuade my [ideal customer persona] to make a purchase with a personalized message."

7. "I'm looking for a cold DM idea that will leverage the authenticity and relatability of my [brand/company] to engage my [ideal customer persona] and persuade them to take [desired action]."

8. "I'm looking for a cold DM idea that will engage my [ideal customer persona] with a unique and exclusive offer and persuade them to take [desired action] with a sense of urgency and exclusivity."

9. "I need a cold DM idea that will create a sense of community and belonging for my [ideal customer

persona] by featuring user-generated content and encouraging them to share their own experiences with my [product/service]."

10. "I need a cold DM idea that will leverage the authenticity and relatability of my [brand/company] to engage my [ideal customer persona] and persuade them to take [desired action] on my [product/service]."

11. "I'm looking for a cold DM idea that will provide a sneak peek of upcoming products or services and create a sense of anticipation and excitement for my [ideal customer persona] with a clear and compelling call-to-action."

12. "I need a cold DM idea that will engage my [ideal customer persona] with a unique and creative visual campaign that showcases the features and benefits of my [product/service] in a compelling way."

13. "I'm looking for a cold DM idea that will leverage the social proof and credibility of my [brand/company] to persuade my [ideal customer persona] to try my [product/service] and share their positive experience with their followers."

14. "I need a cold DM idea that will leverage the authority and expertise of my [brand/company] to educate my [ideal customer persona] on the benefits of my

[product/service] and persuade them to make a purchase."

15. "I'm looking for a cold DM idea that will showcase the unique and personal experiences of my [ideal customer persona] with my [product/service] and persuade them to share their positive review with their followers."

Influencer Marketing Prompts

1. "I'm looking for an influencer marketing campaign outline that will showcase my [product/service] to my [ideal customer persona] and persuade them to take [desired action] with the help of [influencer type] who aligns with our brand values."
2. "I need an influencer marketing campaign outline that will engage my [ideal customer persona] with [specific type of content] from [influencer type] who can showcase the unique features and benefits of our [product/service] in a fun and creative way."
3. "I need an influencer marketing campaign outline that will target my [ideal customer persona] with [specific type of content] from [influencer type] who can authentically share the benefits of our [product/service] and encourage them to make a purchase."
4. "I'm looking for an influencer marketing campaign outline that will leverage the authority and credibility of

[influencer type] to persuade my [ideal customer persona] to try our [product/service] and share their positive experience with their followers."

5. "I need an influencer marketing campaign outline that will leverage the authority and expertise of [influencer type] to educate my [ideal customer persona] on the benefits of our [product/service] and persuade them to make a purchase."

6. "I need an influencer marketing campaign outline that will engage my [ideal customer persona] with [specific type of content] from [influencer type] who can showcase the unique features and benefits of our [product/service] in a compelling and authentic way."

7. "I'm looking for an influencer marketing campaign outline that will leverage the reach and influence of [influencer type] to drive awareness and sales of our [product/service] to my [ideal customer persona]."

8. "I need an influencer marketing campaign outline that will create a sense of urgency and FOMO for my [ideal customer persona] by featuring [influencer type] who can share exclusive deals and promotions for our [product/service]."

9. "I'm looking for an influencer marketing campaign outline that will use the social proof and credibility of [influencer type] to persuade my [ideal customer

persona] to try our [product/service] and share their positive experience with their followers."

10. "I'm looking for an influencer marketing campaign outline that will target my [ideal customer persona] with [specific type of content] from [influencer type] who can provide valuable and relevant information about our [product/service] and encourage them to take [desired action]."

11. "I'm looking for an influencer marketing campaign outline that will use the influence and reach of [influencer type] to drive traffic and sales to our [product/service] for my [ideal customer persona]."

12. "I'm looking for an influencer marketing campaign outline that will leverage the social proof and credibility of [influencer type] to persuade my [ideal customer persona] to try our [product/service] and share their positive experience with their followers."

13. "I need an influencer marketing campaign outline that will use the authenticity and relatability of [influencer type] to engage my [ideal customer persona] and persuade them to take [desired action] on our [product/service]."

14. "I'm looking for an influencer marketing campaign outline that will target my [ideal customer persona] with [specific type of content] from [influencer type] who can

share valuable and relevant information about our [product/service] and encourage them to take [desired action]."

15. "I need an influencer marketing campaign outline that will leverage the authenticity and relatability of [influencer type] to engage my [ideal customer persona] and persuade them to take [desired action] on our [product/service]."

Cold Email Ideas Prompts

1. "I need a cold email idea that will demonstrate how my [product/service] can solve the specific pain points and needs of my [ideal customer persona] in a relatable and engaging way."
2. "I need a cold email idea that will establish credibility and authority with my [ideal customer persona] by showcasing the success stories of previous customers who have used my [product/service]."
3. "I'm looking for a cold email idea that will attract the attention of my [ideal customer persona] and persuade them to take [desired action] with a unique and compelling subject line."
4. "I need a cold email idea that will provide valuable and relevant information to my [ideal customer persona]

about [subject] and persuade them to take [desired action] with a clear and compelling message."

5. "I'm looking for a cold email idea that will draw in my [ideal customer persona] with a relatable and authentic message, and then persuade them to take [desired action] with a strong call-to action and compelling visuals."

6. "I need a cold email idea that will compare my [product/service] to similar options on the market and persuade my [ideal customer persona] to choose us with clear and compelling evidence."

7. "I'm looking for a cold email idea that will overcome objections and concerns my [ideal customer persona] may have about my [product/service] and convince them to take [desired action] with a sense of urgency."

8. "I'm looking for a cold email idea that will establish trust and credibility with my [ideal customer persona] by showcasing the expertise and professionalism of my [company/brand]."

9. "I'm looking for a cold email idea that will provide a step-by-step guide on how to use my [product/service] and persuade my [ideal customer persona] to make a purchase with clear and compelling instructions."

10. "I need a cold email idea that will provide a behind-the-scenes look at my [company/brand] and persuade my

[ideal customer persona] to take [desired action] with a sense of authenticity and relatability."

11. "I need a cold email idea that will use a personalized and targeted approach to engage my [ideal customer persona] and persuade them to take [desired action] with a clear and compelling message."

12. "I need a cold email idea that will engage my [ideal customer persona] with a unique and compelling perspective on [subject] and persuade them to take [desired action] on my [website/product]."

13. "I'm looking for a cold email idea that will showcase the benefits and value of my [product/service] to my [ideal customer persona] and persuade them to make a purchase with a strong call-to action."

14. "I need a cold email idea that will provide a unique and compelling offer to my [ideal customer persona] and persuade them to take [desired action] with a sense of urgency and exclusivity."

15. "I'm looking for a cold email idea that will showcase the unique selling points of my [product/service] and persuade my [ideal customer persona] to make a purchase with a sense of urgency and exclusive offers."

Promotional Social Media Prompts

1. Write a promotional social media post based on the content above.
2. Make promotional social media post for a [product/service].
3. Write a social media announcement about [product/change/launch].
4. Write a social media post that generates leads for [product/service].
5. Write a social media post that drives traffic to [website].
6. Write a social media post promoting [discount/voucher/promotion].
7. Create a promotional social media post for an article about [topic].
8. Write a social media post promoting a [type of event + date].
9. Write a social media post about [product/service] and include [client pain points].
10. Describe the impact of using [product/feature] as a [profession/business].
11. Write X engaging hooks ideas for a social media post about [topic].
12. Craft a social media post for [product/service] that addresses positive customer emotions.

13. Finish this paragraph: We are launching [product name] to help you [benefit].
14. Generate a post announcing the launch of our new product [product name].
15. Create a post highlighting the unique features of our product [product name].
16. Make a post showcasing the benefits of using our product [product name] for [specific problem/issue].
17. Develop a post promoting a limited-time sale or discount for our product [product name].
18. Create a post to encourage customers to leave a review for our product [product name].
19. Generate a post to create a sense of urgency for buying our product [product name].
20. Create a social media post that compares our product [product name] with a similar product on the market.
21. Develop a social media post that features customer testimonials for our product [product name].
22. Make a social media post that demonstrates how our product [product name] can be used in real-life situations.
23. Create a social media post that targets [specific audience] and explains how our product [product name] can help them.

24. Make a social media post listing the benefits of [product/service] for [customer type].
25. Write a PAS for the content above. (Problem, Agitate, Solve)
26. Write an AIDA for the content above. (Attention, Interest, Desire, Action)
27. Write a BAB about the content above. (Before, After, Bridge)

200+ ChatGPT-4 Prompts for Software Developers

Code generation:

1. Generate a boilerplate [language] code for a [class/module/component] named [name] with the following functionality: [functionality description].
2. Create a [language] function to perform [operation] on [data structure] with the following inputs: [input variables] and expected output: [output description].
3. Generate a [language] class for a [domain] application that includes methods for [methods list] and properties [properties list].

4. Based on the [design pattern], create a code snippet in [language] that demonstrates its implementation for a [use case].
5. Write a [language] script to perform [task] using [library/framework] with the following requirements: [requirements list].
6. **Code completion:**
7. In [language], complete the following code snippet that initializes a [data structure] with [values]: [code snippet].
8. Finish the [language] function that calculates [desired output] given the following input parameters: [function signature].
9. Complete the [language] code to make an API call to [API endpoint] with [parameters] and process the response: [code snippet].
10. Fill in the missing [language] code to implement error handling for the following function: [code snippet].
11. Complete the following [language] loop that iterates over [data structure] and performs [operation]: [code snippet].
12. **Bug detection:**
13. Identify any potential bugs in the following [language] code snippet: [code snippet].
14. Analyze the given [language] code and suggest improvements to prevent [error type]: [code snippet].

15. Find any memory leaks in the following [language] code and suggest fixes: [code snippet].
16. Check for any race conditions or concurrency issues in the given [language] code: [code snippet].
17. Review the following [language] code for any security vulnerabilities: [code snippet].
18. **Code review:**
19. Review the following [language] code for best practices and suggest improvements: [code snippet].
20. Analyze the given [language] code for adherence to [coding style guidelines]: [code snippet].
21. Check the following [language] code for proper error handling and suggest enhancements: [code snippet].
22. Evaluate the modularity and maintainability of the given [language] code: [code snippet].
23. Assess the performance of the following [language] code and provide optimization suggestions: [code snippet].
24. **Natural language processing:**
25. Perform sentiment analysis on the following text: [text sample].
26. Extract named entities from the following text: [text sample].
27. Summarize the following article/document: [URL or text sample].

28. Identify the main topic(s) of the following text: [text sample].
29. Perform keyword extraction on the following text: [text sample].
30. **API documentation generation:**
31. Generate API documentation for the following [language] code: [code snippet].
32. Create a concise API reference for the given [language] class: [code snippet].
33. Generate usage examples for the following [language] API: [code snippet].
34. Document the expected input and output for the given [language] function: [code snippet].
35. Produce a quick-start guide for using the following [language] library: [code snippet].
36. **Query optimization:**
37. Optimize the following SQL query for better performance: [SQL query].
38. Analyze the given SQL query for any potential bottlenecks: [SQL query].
39. Suggest indexing strategies for the following SQL query: [SQL query].
40. Rewrite the following SQL query to use JOINs instead of subqueries for improved performance: [SQL query].

41. Optimize the following NoSQL query for better performance and resource usage: [NoSQL query].
42. Identify any inefficiencies in the given database schema that may be affecting query performance: [schema description].
43. Suggest partitioning or sharding strategies for the following large-scale database query: [SQL or NoSQL query].
44. Compare the performance of the given SQL query using different database engines (e.g., MySQL, PostgreSQL, Oracle): [SQL query].
45. **Chatbots and conversational AI:**
46. Create a conversational flow for a customer support chatbot that handles [issue or inquiry type].
47. Design a chatbot interaction that helps users find [product or service] based on their preferences and requirements.
48. Develop a conversational script for a chatbot that guides users through the [onboarding process or feature setup].
49. Implement a chatbot that can answer frequently asked questions about [topic or domain].
50. Create a natural language interface for a chatbot that allows users to perform [specific task or operation] using voice commands or text input.
51. **User interface design:**

52. Generate a UI mockup for a [web/mobile] application that focuses on [user goal or task].
53. Suggest improvements to the existing user interface of [app or website] to enhance [usability, accessibility, or aesthetics].
54. Design a responsive user interface for a [web/mobile] app that adapts to different screen sizes and orientations.
55. Create a wireframe for a [web/mobile] app that streamlines user workflows for [specific use case].
56. Design a UI component library for a [web/mobile] app that adheres to [design system or style guide].
57. **Automated testing:**
58. Generate test cases for the following [language] function based on the input parameters and expected output: [function signature].
59. Create a test script for the given [language] code that covers [unit/integration/system] testing: [code snippet].
60. Generate test data for the following [language] function that tests various edge cases: [function signature].
61. Design a testing strategy for a [web/mobile] app that includes [unit, integration, system, and/or performance] testing.

62. Write a test suite for a [language] API that verifies its functionality and performance under different conditions.
63. **Code refactoring:**
64. Suggest refactoring improvements for the following [language] code to enhance readability and maintainability: [code snippet].
65. Identify opportunities to apply [design pattern] in the given [language] code: [code snippet].
66. Optimize the following [language] code for better performance: [code snippet].
67. Refactor the given [language] code to improve its modularity and reusability: [code snippet].
68. Propose changes to the given [language] code to adhere to [coding style or best practices]: [code snippet].
69. **Algorithm development:**
70. Suggest an optimal algorithm to solve the following problem: [problem description].
71. Improve the efficiency of the given algorithm for [specific use case]: [algorithm or pseudocode].
72. Design an algorithm that can handle [large-scale data or high-throughput] for [specific task or operation].
73. Propose a parallel or distributed version of the following algorithm to improve performance: [algorithm or pseudocode].

74. Evaluate the time and space complexity of the given algorithm and suggest optimizations: [algorithm or pseudocode].

75. **Code translation:**
76. Translate the following [source language] code to [target language]: [code snippet].
77. Convert the given [source language] class or module to [target language] while preserving its functionality and structure: [code snippet].
78. Migrate the following [source language] code that uses [library or framework] to [target language] with a similar library or framework: [code snippet].
79. Rewrite the given [source language] algorithm in [target language] with equivalent performance characteristics: [algorithm or pseudocode].
80. Adapt the following [source language] code snippet to [target language] while adhering to [target language's best practices]: [code snippet].
81. Translate the given [source language] function that handles [specific task or operation] to [target language]: [code snippet].

82. **Personalized learning:**
83. Curate a list of resources to learn [programming language or technology] based on my current skill level: [beginner/intermediate/advanced].

84. Recommend a learning path to become proficient in [specific programming domain or technology] considering my background in [existing skills or experience].
85. Suggest project ideas or coding exercises to practice and improve my skills in [programming language or technology].
86. Recommend online courses, tutorials, or books that focus on [specific topic or concept] in [programming language or technology].
87. Identify areas of improvement in my coding skills based on the following [language] code: [code snippet].
88. **Technical writing:**
89. Write a tutorial on how to implement [specific feature or functionality] using [programming language or technology].
90. Create a step-by-step guide on setting up and configuring [tool or software] for [specific use case or environment].
91. Draft a README file for a [programming language or technology] project that includes an overview, installation instructions, and usage examples.
92. Write a clear and concise explanation of the [algorithm or concept] in [programming language or technology].

93. Create a troubleshooting guide for common issues and their solutions when working with [programming language, library, or framework].
94. **Requirement analysis:**
95. Interpret the following project requirements and suggest a high-level architecture or design: [requirements description].
96. Identify potential risks or challenges in implementing the given project requirements: [requirements description].
97. Suggest a prioritization strategy for the following list of project requirements: [requirements list].
98. Based on the given project requirements, recommend a suitable [programming language, framework, or technology]: [requirements description].
99. Estimate the development effort and resources needed to implement the following project requirements: [requirements description].
100. **Project planning:**
101. Estimate the timeline and milestones for a project with the following requirements: [requirements description].
102. Propose a development methodology (e.g., Agile, Scrum, Waterfall) for a project with the following characteristics: [project description].
103. Suggest a team structure and roles for a project with the following scope and requirements: [project description].

104. Identify dependencies and potential bottlenecks in a project with the following requirements and constraints: [requirements description].
105. Develop a high-level project plan that includes tasks, resources, and timelines for a project with the following objectives: [project objectives].
106. **Issue tracking and resolution:**
107. Automatically categorize and prioritize the following list of reported issues: [issue list].
108. Suggest potential solutions for the following reported issue: [issue description].
109. Identify the root cause of the given issue and propose steps to prevent its recurrence: [issue description].
110. Estimate the effort required to resolve the following issue and its impact on the project timeline: [issue description].
111. Propose a workaround or temporary fix for the following critical issue while a permanent solution is being developed: [issue description].
112. **Code visualization:**
113. Generate a UML diagram for the following [language] code: [code snippet].
114. Create a flowchart or visual representation of the given [language] algorithm: [algorithm or pseudocode].

115. Visualize the call graph or dependencies of the following [language] code: [code snippet].
116. Generate a data flow diagram for the given [language] code that demonstrates how data is processed: [code snippet].
117. Create an interactive visualization of the runtime behavior or performance of the following [language] code: [code snippet].
118. **Data visualization:**
119. Generate a bar chart that represents the following data: [data or dataset description].
120. Create a line chart that visualizes the trend in the following time series data: [data or dataset description].
121. Design a heatmap that represents the correlation between the following variables: [variable list].
122. Visualize the distribution of the following dataset using a histogram or box plot: [data or dataset description].
123. Generate a scatter plot that demonstrates the relationship between the following two variables: [variable 1] and [variable 2].
124. **Prototyping:**
125. Generate a proof-of-concept [language] code for a [project idea or feature] based on the following requirements: [requirements description].

126. Create a functional prototype of a [web/mobile] app that demonstrates [specific functionality or user flow].
127. Develop a minimal viable product (MVP) for a [product or service] based on the following specifications: [specifications description].
128. Implement a simple simulation or model of a [system or process] using [language or technology].
129. Create a working demo of a [tool or feature] that showcases its potential benefits and use cases.
130. **Collaborative coding:**
131. Facilitate a code review session between [team member 1] and [team member 2] for the following [language] code: [code snippet].
132. Set up a pair programming session between [team member 1] and [team member 2] to implement [specific feature or functionality].
133. Organize a brainstorming session to generate ideas and solutions for [problem or challenge] faced by the development team.
134. Help establish a communication channel between [team member 1] and [team member 2] to discuss and resolve [technical issue or question].
135. Assist in coordinating a code merge or integration between [team member 1]'s work and [team member 2]'s work.

136. **Code analytics:**
137. Analyze the given codebase to identify frequently used libraries or dependencies: [repository URL or codebase description].
138. Generate a report on the complexity and maintainability of the following codebase: [repository URL or codebase description].
139. Identify trends or patterns in the development history of the given codebase: [repository URL or codebase description].
140. Analyze the codebase to identify potential areas of improvement or refactoring: [repository URL or codebase description].
141. Generate a summary of the coding styles and conventions used in the given codebase: [repository URL or codebase description].
142. **Design pattern suggestions:**
143. Based on the given [language] code, recommend a suitable design pattern to improve its structure: [code snippet].
144. Identify opportunities to apply the [design pattern] in the following [language] codebase: [repository URL or codebase description].

Generative AI: Unleashing Creative Genius with Prompt Engineering

145. Suggest an alternative design pattern for the given [language] code that may provide additional benefits: [code snippet].
146. Explain how the [design pattern] can be applied in the given [language] code to address [specific issue or challenge]: [code snippet].
147. Compare the pros and cons of using [design pattern 1] vs [design pattern 2] in the context of the given [language] code: [code snippet].
148. Provide examples of implementing the [design pattern] in [language] for the following scenarios: [scenario list].
149. Suggest a design pattern to optimize the performance of the given [language] code handling [specific task or operation]: [code snippet].
150. Evaluate the effectiveness of the [design pattern] in addressing the specific requirements or constraints of the given [language] code: [code snippet].
151. Propose a combination of design patterns that can be used to enhance the given [language] code's architecture and functionality: [code snippet].
152. **Performance optimization:**
153. Identify performance bottlenecks in the given [language] code and suggest optimizations: [code snippet].
154. Propose changes to the given [language] code to improve its memory usage: [code snippet].

155. Suggest ways to parallelize or distribute the following [language] code to improve its performance: [code snippet].
156. Compare the performance of the given [language] code using different optimization techniques or libraries: [code snippet].
157. Analyze the performance of the following [language] code in different environments or hardware configurations: [code snippet].
158. **Security and privacy:**
159. Evaluate the security of the given [language] code and suggest improvements: [code snippet].
160. Identify potential privacy risks in the following [language] code and recommend mitigation strategies: [code snippet].
161. Propose changes to the given [language] code to improve its resistance to common security threats (e.g., SQL injection, XSS, CSRF): [code snippet].
162. Analyze the security of the given [language] code in the context of [specific industry standards or regulations]: [code snippet].
163. Suggest encryption or hashing algorithms to secure sensitive data in the given [language] code: [code snippet].
164. **Accessibility and inclusivity:**

165. Evaluate the accessibility of the given [web/mobile] app and suggest improvements to comply with WCAG guidelines: [app URL or description].
166. Propose changes to the given [web/mobile] app to improve its usability for users with [specific disability or impairment]: [app URL or description].
167. Suggest ways to make the given [web/mobile] app more inclusive and diverse in terms of content, imagery, and language: [app URL or description].
168. Analyze the accessibility of the given [web/mobile] app on various devices and screen sizes: [app URL or description].
169. Recommend tools or libraries to help improve the accessibility and inclusivity of the given [web/mobile] app: [app URL or description].
170. **DevOps and CI/CD:**
171. Design a CI/CD pipeline for the given [language] project based on its requirements and constraints: [project description].
172. Propose a strategy to automate the deployment of the given [language] application to [cloud provider or environment]: [app description].
173. Suggest improvements to the given [language] project's build and deployment process to increase efficiency: [project description].

174. Compare the advantages and disadvantages of different containerization technologies (e.g., Docker, Kubernetes, Podman) for the given [language] project: [project description].
175. Identify opportunities to optimize the given [language] project's infrastructure and resource usage using cloud-native technologies: [project description].
176. **Remote work and collaboration:**
177. Suggest tools and best practices for remote collaboration among the members of a [language] development team.
178. Propose strategies to improve communication and coordination between distributed team members working on a [language] project.
179. Recommend a workflow for managing and prioritizing tasks for a remote [language] development team.
180. Suggest ways to maintain team morale and motivation among remote [language] developers during a long-term project.
181. Share tips for organizing and facilitating effective remote meetings for a [language] development team.
182. Propose techniques for remote pair programming and code review sessions among distributed [language] developers.
183. **Open-source contribution:**

184. Identify suitable open-source [language] projects for a developer with [specific skills or interests].
185. Suggest open issues or feature requests in the following [language] open-source project that match my skill set: [repository URL or project description].
186. Recommend best practices for contributing to [language] open-source projects as a new or inexperienced contributor.
187. Provide guidance on navigating the codebase and development process of the given [language] open-source project: [repository URL or project description].
188. Explain how to prepare and submit a pull request for the given [language] open-source project: [repository URL or project description].
189. **Technical documentation:**
190. Write an API reference for the following [language] code: [code snippet].
191. Create a user guide for the given [software or tool] that covers installation, configuration, and basic usage.
192. Write a comprehensive test plan for the given [language] code, including test cases and scenarios: [code snippet].
193. Develop a FAQ section that addresses common questions and issues related to the given [language] project or tool.

194. Produce a clear and concise overview of the architecture and design of the given [language] project or system: [project description].

195. API design and development:

196. Design an API for a [type of application or service] that supports the following operations: [list of operations].
197. Propose a RESTful API structure for the given [language] code that follows best practices: [code snippet].
198. Suggest improvements to the following API design to enhance its usability, performance, or security: [API description].
199. Write a [language] code to interact with the following API: [API documentation or reference].
200. Compare different API authentication and authorization mechanisms (e.g., OAuth, JWT, API keys) for the given [language] project: [project description].

201. Integration and interoperability:

202. Suggest a strategy for integrating the given [language] code with [external system or API]: [code snippet].
203. Identify potential challenges and solutions for interoperability between the following systems or technologies: [system or technology list].
204. Propose a data transformation or mapping solution for the given [language] code to interface with [external data source or format]: [code snippet].

205. Recommend best practices for building and maintaining a [language] codebase that integrates with multiple third-party services or APIs.
206. Evaluate the compatibility and performance of the given [language] code when interacting with [specific technology or platform]: [code snippet].

207. **Technical interview preparation:**

208. Suggest [language] coding exercises or challenges to practice for a technical interview.
209. Share tips and advice on how to approach and solve [language] coding problems during a technical interview.
210. Provide examples of common [language] technical interview questions and their solutions.
211. Conduct a mock [language] technical interview, including problem-solving, coding, and explanation of thought process.
212. Evaluate and provide feedback on my performance during a [language] technical interview, including areas for improvement and strengths.

213. **Code generation and scaffolding:**

214. Generate a [language] code template for a [type of application or service] that follows best practices: [application or service description].
215. Create a boilerplate [language] project structure for a [type of application] that includes necessary

configuration files and dependencies: [application description].

216. Suggest a code scaffolding tool or library for the given [language] that helps streamline the development process.
217. Generate a CRUD (Create, Read, Update, Delete) [language] code for a [type of application or service] that interacts with a [type of database]: [application or service description].
218. Provide a [language] code snippet that demonstrates the usage of a [library or framework] to build a [specific feature or functionality]: [library or framework name].
219. **Technical leadership and mentoring:**
220. Share best practices for leading and managing a [language] development team.
221. Suggest strategies for mentoring and coaching junior [language] developers to help them grow and succeed.
222. Propose techniques for creating a culture of continuous learning and improvement within a [language] development team.
223. Recommend approaches to balancing technical debt and feature development in a [language] project.
224. Share advice on how to effectively communicate technical decisions and trade-offs to non-technical stakeholders.

225. **Code readability and style:**
226. Evaluate the readability of the given [language] code and suggest improvements: [code snippet].
227. Propose a consistent coding style for the given [language] code that aligns with best practices: [code snippet].
228. Compare different [language] code formatting tools or linters and recommend one that best suits the given project: [project description].
229. Suggest ways to refactor the given [language] code to make it more concise and maintainable: [code snippet].
230. Share advice on how to write clean and self-documenting [language] code that is easy for others to understand and maintain.
231. **Career advice for software developers:**
232. Recommend strategies for building a strong and diverse [language] development skill set.
233. Share advice on how to create an effective and compelling software developer portfolio.
234. Suggest networking opportunities or resources for [language] developers to connect with peers and potential employers.
235. Provide tips for negotiating a job offer or promotion as a [language] developer.

236. Share advice on how to transition from a different technical role to a [language] development role.

237. Developer productivity:

238. Recommend tools and techniques to improve productivity for a [language] developer.
239. Suggest ways to minimize distractions and maintain focus during [language] development tasks.
240. Share strategies for effectively managing and prioritizing tasks in a [language] development project.
241. Propose techniques for estimating and tracking the time required for various [language] development tasks.
242. Provide advice on how to maintain a healthy work-life balance as a [language] developer.

243. Testing and quality assurance:

244. Design a test suite for the given [language] code that covers various test scenarios and edge cases: [code snippet].
245. Recommend best practices for writing and maintaining unit tests for a [language] codebase.
246. Suggest strategies for automating regression testing in the given [language] project: [project description].
247. Compare different [language] testing frameworks and recommend one that best suits the given project: [project description].

248. Share advice on how to incorporate continuous testing and quality assurance into the development process for a [language] project.

1. **Learning a new language**
2. What is the most effective way to learn a new language for business purposes?
3. Can you recommend some free resources for learning [language] online?
4. How long does it take to become proficient in [language], and what are the best methods for retaining information?
5. What are some tips for practicing conversation in [language] with native speakers?
6. What are some common pitfalls to avoid when learning a new language?

7. **Improving writing skills**
8. How can I improve the clarity and concision of my writing?
9. What are some techniques for crafting compelling headlines that grab readers' attention?
10. Can you provide feedback on my writing sample and suggest areas for improvement?

11. How can I develop my own writing style and voice?
12. What are some common grammar and syntax errors to watch out for when writing?

13. **Enhancing communication skills**
14. What are some effective communication strategies for virtual teams?
15. Can you provide tips for communicating with difficult coworkers or clients?
16. What are some ways to convey complex information to a non-technical audience?
17. How can I improve my active listening skills?
18. What are some ways to build rapport and trust with colleagues?

19. **Building confidence**
20. What are some ways to overcome imposter syndrome and feel more confident in my abilities?
21. Can you provide some exercises for building self-esteem and self-worth?
22. How can I project more confidence in my body language and tone of voice?
23. What are some common beliefs or behaviors that undermine confidence, and how can I avoid them?

24. How can I turn my mistakes or failures into learning opportunities and grow more confident as a result?

25. **Improving public speaking skills**
26. How can I overcome my fear of public speaking and deliver effective presentations?
27. Can you provide tips for engaging my audience and keeping their attention during a speech?
28. What are some ways to use storytelling to make my presentations more impactful?
29. How can I develop my own speaking style and voice?
30. What are some common mistakes to avoid when delivering a speech?

31. **Improving grammar and syntax**
32. What are some common grammar and syntax errors to watch out for when writing?
33. Can you provide some exercises or resources for improving my grammar and syntax skills?
34. How can I identify and correct errors in my writing more effectively?
35. What are some common punctuation errors to avoid when writing?
36. How can I improve my sentence structure and clarity?

37. **Writing better emails**
38. How can I write more effective emails that get my point across clearly and concisely?
39. Can you provide examples of good email etiquette and best practices?
40. How can I use email to build relationships and maintain connections with colleagues and clients?
41. What are some common mistakes to avoid when writing emails?
42. How can I ensure that my emails are professional and appropriate in different contexts?

43. **Writing more compelling stories**
44. How can I craft stories that are engaging and memorable?
45. Can you provide tips for developing characters and plotlines that resonate with readers?
46. How can I use storytelling to communicate my message more effectively?
47. What are some common mistakes to avoid when writing stories?
48. How can I find my own unique voice and style as a writer?

49. **Improving creativity and imagination**
50. What are some exercises or techniques for stimulating my creativity and imagination?
51. How can I overcome creative blocks and generate new ideas more consistently?
52. Can you provide examples of creative problem-solving in a business context?
53. How can I incorporate more creativity into my work and daily life?
54. What are some common misconceptions about creativity, and how can I avoid them?

55. **Generating new ideas**
56. What are some methods for generating new ideas and solutions to problems?
57. Can you provide examples of innovative businesses and products that have emerged from creative ideation processes?
58. How can I evaluate the feasibility and potential impact of new ideas?
59. What are some common obstacles to generating new ideas, and how can I overcome them?
60. How can I involve others in the ideation process and leverage diverse perspectives?
61. **Enhancing critical thinking skills**

62. What are some exercises or resources for developing my critical thinking skills?
63. Can you provide examples of how critical thinking can be applied in a business context?
64. How can I evaluate arguments and evidence more effectively?
65. What are some common cognitive biases to watch out for when thinking critically?
66. How can I use critical thinking to make better decisions and solve problems more effectively?

67. **Developing problem-solving skills**
68. What are some frameworks or methodologies for approaching problems systematically?
69. Can you provide examples of effective problem-solving in a business context?
70. How can I identify the root causes of problems and develop solutions that address them?
71. What are some common barriers to effective problem-solving, and how can I overcome them?
72. How can I involve others in the problem-solving process and leverage diverse perspectives?

73. **Improving decision-making skills**
74. What are some strategies for making more informed and effective decisions?
75. Can you provide examples of how decision-making processes can vary across different industries or contexts?
76. How can I weigh the pros and cons of different options more effectively?
77. What are some common cognitive biases to watch out for when making decisions?
78. How can I involve others in the decision-making process and leverage diverse perspectives?
79. **Enhancing memory and recall**
80. What are some techniques or exercises for improving my memory and recall?
81. Can you provide examples of how memory skills can be useful in a business context?
82. How can I retain information more effectively when studying or learning new material?
83. What are some common obstacles to memory and recall, and how can I overcome them?
84. How can I incorporate memory techniques into my daily life to improve productivity and effectiveness?

85. **Improving time management skills**
86. What are some strategies for managing my time more effectively?
87. Can you provide examples of time management tools or techniques that can help me stay organized?
88. How can I prioritize my tasks and responsibilities to maximize my productivity?
89. What are some common time-wasters to avoid, and how can I minimize their impact?
90. How can I balance competing demands on my time, such as work, family, and personal interests?

91. **Developing leadership skills**
92. What are some characteristics of effective leaders, and how can I cultivate them in myself?
93. Can you provide examples of leadership styles and how they can be applied in different contexts?
94. How can I build and maintain relationships with my team members and colleagues?
95. What are some common challenges that leaders face, and how can I address them?
96. How can I motivate and inspire others to achieve their goals?

97. **Improving communication skills**
98. What are some techniques or resources for improving my communication skills, both verbal and written?
99. Can you provide examples of effective communication in a business context?
100. How can I adapt my communication style to different audiences and situations?
101. What are some common communication barriers to watch out for, and how can I overcome them?
102. How can I provide constructive feedback and resolve conflicts in a productive manner?

103. **Enhancing emotional intelligence**
104. What is emotional intelligence, and why is it important in the workplace?
105. Can you provide examples of how emotional intelligence can be applied in a business context?
106. How can I develop my own emotional intelligence skills, such as self-awareness, empathy, and relationship management?
107. What are some common misconceptions about emotional intelligence, and how can I avoid them?

108. How can I use emotional intelligence to build stronger relationships and achieve better outcomes in my work and personal life?

109. **Improving public speaking skills**
110. What are some techniques or resources for improving my public speaking skills?
111. Can you provide examples of effective public speaking in a business context?
112. How can I prepare and deliver a compelling presentation that engages my audience?
113. What are some common mistakes to avoid when speaking in public?
114. How can I build my confidence and overcome anxiety when speaking in front of a group?

115. **Developing networking skills**
116. What are some strategies for building and maintaining a professional network?
117. Can you provide examples of effective networking in a business context?
118. How can I approach networking events and interactions with confidence and purpose?
119. What are some common misconceptions about networking, and how can I avoid them?

120. How can I leverage my network to achieve my professional and personal goals?

121. Setting and achieving goals
122. How can I set SMART goals that align with my personal and professional aspirations?
123. Can you provide examples of effective goal-setting in a business context?
124. How can I stay motivated and accountable as I work towards my goals?
125. What are some common obstacles to goal achievement, and how can I overcome them?
126. How can I celebrate my successes and learn from my failures along the way?

127. Improving critical thinking skills
128. What is critical thinking, and why is it important in the workplace?
129. Can you provide examples of critical thinking in a business context?
130. How can I develop my own critical thinking skills, such as analysis, synthesis, and evaluation?
131. What are some common biases and fallacies to watch out for when making decisions or solving problems?

132. How can I use critical thinking to generate creative solutions and make informed decisions?

133. **Enhancing creativity**
134. What is creativity, and why is it important in the workplace?
135. Can you provide examples of creativity in a business context?
136. How can I cultivate my own creativity and generate new ideas?
137. What are some common obstacles to creativity, and how can I overcome them?
138. How can I use creative thinking to solve problems and innovate in my work and personal life?

139. **Developing a growth mindset**
140. What is a growth mindset, and how does it differ from a fixed mindset?
141. Can you provide examples of growth mindset in a business context?
142. How can I develop and maintain a growth mindset, even in the face of challenges and setbacks?
143. What are some common misconceptions about intelligence and talent, and how can I avoid them?

144. How can I use a growth mindset to achieve my personal and professional goals?

145. **Improving decision-making skills**
146. What are some techniques or frameworks for making effective decisions in a business context?
147. Can you provide examples of decision-making in a business context?
148. How can I weigh the pros and cons of different options and select the best course of action?
149. What are some common decision-making biases to watch out for, and how can I avoid them?
150. How can I make decisions with confidence and avoid second-guessing myself?

151. **Enhancing financial literacy**
152. What are some key financial concepts that are important for me to understand in a business context?
153. Can you provide examples of financial analysis and decision-making in a business context?
154. How can I improve my own financial literacy and make informed decisions about investments, budgeting, and debt management?

155. What are some common financial mistakes to avoid, and how can I minimize my financial risk?
156. How can I use financial knowledge to achieve my personal and professional goals?

157. **Improving teamwork skills**
158. What are some strategies for building and maintaining effective teams in a business context?
159. Can you provide examples of successful team collaborations and projects?
160. How can I contribute to a positive team culture and resolve conflicts in a productive manner?
161. What are some common challenges that teams face, and how can I address them?
162. How can I use teamwork skills to achieve better outcomes in my work and personal life?

163. **Developing project management skills**
164. What are some key principles and techniques for effective project management in a business context?
165. Can you provide examples of successful project management in a business context?
166. How can I plan and execute projects that are on time, on budget, and meet stakeholder expectations?

167. What are some common project management pitfalls to avoid, and how can I mitigate risks?
168. How can I use project management skills to achieve my personal and professional goals?

169. **Improving negotiation skills**
170. What are some strategies for successful negotiation in a business context?
171. Can you provide examples of successful negotiations and outcomes?
172. How can I prepare for and conduct effective negotiations with clients, vendors, and colleagues?

173. **Developing leadership skills**
174. What are some key traits and behaviors of effective leaders in a business context?
175. Can you provide examples of successful leadership in a business context?
176. How can I develop my own leadership skills and cultivate a positive leadership style?
177. What are some common leadership challenges and how can I address them?
178. How can I use leadership skills to achieve my personal and professional goals?

179. **Enhancing emotional intelligence**
180. What is emotional intelligence, and why is it important in the workplace?
181. Can you provide examples of emotional intelligence in a business context?
182. How can I develop my own emotional intelligence, including self-awareness, self-regulation, empathy, and social skills?
183. What are some common emotional challenges that arise in the workplace, and how can I address them?
184. How can I use emotional intelligence to build better relationships and achieve better outcomes in my work and personal life?

185. **Improving communication skills**
186. What are some strategies for effective communication in a business context, including verbal and written communication?
187. Can you provide examples of successful communication in a business context?
188. How can I tailor my communication style to different audiences and situations?
189. What are some common communication barriers and how can I overcome them?

190. How can I use communication skills to build better relationships and achieve better outcomes in my work and personal life?

191. **Enhancing time management skills**
192. What are some strategies for effective time management in a business context?
193. Can you provide examples of successful time management in a business context?
194. How can I prioritize tasks and activities to maximize productivity and achieve my goals?
195. What are some common time management pitfalls to avoid, and how can I overcome them?
196. How can I use time management skills to achieve better outcomes in my work and personal life?

197. **Improving customer service skills**
198. What are some strategies for providing excellent customer service in a business context?
199. Can you provide examples of successful customer service interactions?
200. How can I handle difficult or upset customers in a professional and empathetic manner?
201. What are some common customer service challenges and how can I address them?

202. How can I use customer service skills to build better relationships and achieve better outcomes in my work and personal life?

203. **Developing public speaking skills**
204. What are some techniques for delivering effective presentations in a business context?
205. Can you provide examples of successful public speaking in a business context?
206. How can I prepare and practice for public speaking opportunities, including speeches, pitches, and meetings?
207. What are some common public speaking challenges and how can I overcome them?
208. How can I use public speaking skills to build my professional reputation and achieve better outcomes in my work and personal life?

209. **Enhancing networking skills**
210. What are some strategies for building and maintaining professional networks in a business context?
211. Can you provide examples of successful networking interactions and outcomes?

212. How can I approach networking opportunities in a confident and authentic manner?
213. What are some common networking challenges and how can I address them?
214. How can I use networking skills to build my professional reputation and achieve better outcomes in my work and personal life?

215. **Improving technology skills**
216. What are some key technology concepts and tools that are important to understand in a business context?
217. Can you provide examples of successful technology implementations and outcomes?
218. How can I improve my own technology skills and stay up-to-date with emerging trends and developments?
219. What are some common technology challenges and how can I address them?
220. How can I use technology skills to enhance my productivity and achieve better outcomes in my work and personal life?

221. **Developing creativity and innovation**
222. What are some strategies for fostering creativity and innovation in a business context?
223. Can you provide examples of successful creative and innovative initiatives?
224. How can I cultivate a mindset of curiosity and experimentation?
225. What are some common barriers to creativity and innovation, and how can I overcome them?
226. How can I use creativity and innovation to drive business growth and achieve better outcomes in my work and personal life?

227. **Improving financial literacy**
228. What are some key financial concepts and tools that are important to understand in a business context?
229. Can you provide examples of successful financial management and outcomes?
230. How can I improve my own financial literacy and make informed decisions about investments, expenses, and revenue?
231. What are some common financial challenges and how can I address them?

232. How can I use financial knowledge to drive business growth and achieve better outcomes in my work and personal life?

233. **Enhancing problem-solving skills**
234. What are some strategies for effective problem-solving in a business context?
235. Can you provide examples of successful problem-solving initiatives?
236. How can I approach complex problems with a structured and analytical mindset?
237. What are some common problem-solving challenges and how can I overcome them?
238. How can I use problem-solving skills to drive innovation and achieve better outcomes in my work and personal life?

100+ GPT-4 Prompts To Make Money Online

1. What are the biggest trends in [industry/vertical] and how can we leverage them to grow [our business]?
2. How can we gather insights on our [target audience's] preferences and behaviors to inform our product development strategy?

3. What are our [competitors] doing that we're not, and how can we stay ahead of the curve?
4. Can you create a list of [product/service] keywords that are frequently searched by our target audience?
5. How can we analyze customer feedback to identify areas for improvement in our [product/service]?

6. **Content creation**
7. Can you write a blog post on [topic] that will resonate with our [target audience]?
8. How can we create social media posts that will generate engagement and drive traffic to our [website]?
9. Can you write a product review that highlights the benefits of our [product/service]?
10. How can we create compelling email marketing content that will drive conversions?
11. How can we create video content that will appeal to our [target audience] and generate views?

12. **Search engine optimization**
13. How can we improve our website's organic search rankings for [keyword/phrase]?
14. Can you provide recommendations for optimizing our website's on-page SEO?

15. How can we improve our website's loading speed to improve our search engine rankings?
16. How can we optimize our Google My Business listing to improve our local search presence?
17. How can we optimize our website's mobile experience for improved search engine rankings?

18. **Social media marketing**
19. Can you create a social media content calendar that aligns with our overall marketing strategy?
20. How can we increase our social media engagement and followers?
21. Can you create a social media ad campaign that will generate conversions?
22. How can we use social media to drive traffic to our website?
23. How can we use social media to build brand awareness and credibility?

24. **Ad copy creation**
25. How can we create ad copy that speaks directly to our target audience and generates clicks?
26. Can you create a Facebook ad that highlights the benefits of our [product/service]?

27. How can we create ad copy that differentiates us from our competitors?
28. How can we use ad copy to generate leads and drive conversions?
29. How can we use ad copy to build brand awareness and credibility?

30. **Lead generation**
31. How can we generate leads for our [product/service] using social media?
32. Can you create a lead magnet that will generate interest in our [product/service]?
33. How can we optimize our landing pages to generate more leads?
34. Can you create a lead scoring system to prioritize our leads and improve our sales team's efficiency?
35. How can we use email marketing to generate leads and move them down the funnel?
36. How can we use paid search ads to generate leads and drive conversions?
37. How can we use content marketing to generate leads and build brand awareness?

38. **Customer service**
39. How can we use chatbots to improve our customer service and response time?
40. Can you create canned responses that our customer service team can use to improve efficiency?
41. How can we use customer feedback to improve our customer service experience?
42. How can we use social media to improve our customer service and address customer complaints?
43. How can we create a customer loyalty program that rewards our most loyal customers?

44. **Competitor analysis**
45. How can we analyze our competitors' website traffic and identify areas for improvement?
46. Can you create a competitive analysis report that compares our [product/service] to our competitors' offerings?
47. How can we use social media to monitor our competitors' activity and stay ahead of the curve?
48. How can we use competitive analysis to identify gaps in the market and improve our product offerings?
49. How can we use competitive analysis to differentiate ourselves from our competitors and improve our positioning?

50. **Reputation management**
51. How can we monitor our online reputation and respond to negative reviews?
52. Can you create a reputation management strategy that improves our online credibility and brand image?
53. How can we use customer testimonials to improve our online reputation?
54. How can we use social media to improve our online reputation and engage with our customers?
55. How can we use SEO to improve our online reputation and suppress negative search results?

56. **Brand voice development**
57. How can we create a brand voice that resonates with our target audience and differentiates us from our competitors?
58. Can you create a brand style guide that defines our brand voice, tone, and messaging?
59. How can we use storytelling to reinforce our brand voice and build brand loyalty?
60. How can we use humor to inject personality into our brand voice and generate engagement?

61. How can we use user-generated content to reinforce our brand voice and build community?

62. **Website copy optimization**
63. How can we optimize our website's copy to improve user experience and drive conversions?
64. Can you create a landing page that highlights the benefits of our [product/service] and generates conversions?
65. How can we use persuasive language and calls-to-action to improve our website's copy?
66. How can we use storytelling to improve our website's copy and build brand loyalty?
67. How can we use data to inform our website's copy and improve its effectiveness?

68. **Landing page optimization**
69. How can we optimize our [landing pages] to improve conversion rates?
70. Can you create a landing page that aligns with our [overall marketing strategy] and generates leads?
71. How can we use A/B testing to optimize our [landing pages] and improve conversion rates?
72. How can we use data analysis to identify areas for improvement on our [landing pages]?

73. How can we use persuasive language and design elements to improve our [landing pages' effectiveness]?

74. **Customer persona creation**
75. How can we create customer personas that accurately represent our [target audience]?
76. Can you create a customer persona that aligns with our [ideal customer profile]?
77. How can we use [customer personas] to inform our product development strategy?
78. How can we use [customer personas] to improve our marketing messaging and generate more conversions?
79. How can we use customer personas to improve our [customer service and response time]?

80. **Product naming**
81. How can we create a product name that accurately reflects our [brand] and resonates with our target audience?
82. Can you provide recommendations for a product name that is memorable and easy to pronounce?
83. How can we use SEO to optimize our product name for search engines and improve our online visibility?

84. How can we use data analysis to inform our product name and ensure it resonates with our target audience?
85. Can you create a naming strategy that aligns with our brand voice and values?
86. How can we use user testing to gather feedback on potential product names and make informed decisions?

87. **Social media strategy**
88. How can we use social media to build brand awareness and engage with our target audience?
89. Can you create a social media strategy that aligns with our overall marketing goals and objectives?
90. How can we use social media to generate leads and drive conversions?
91. How can we use social media to monitor brand mentions and address customer complaints?
92. How can we use data analysis to measure the effectiveness of our social media strategy and make informed decisions?

93. **Video marketing**
94. How can we use video marketing to improve our online visibility and engage with our target audience?
95. Can you create a video marketing campaign that aligns with our overall marketing goals and objectives?
96. How can we use video marketing to generate leads and drive conversions?
97. How can we use data analysis to measure the effectiveness of our video marketing campaigns and make informed decisions?
98. How can we use storytelling to improve the effectiveness of our video marketing campaigns and build brand loyalty?

99. **Influencer marketing**
100. How can we use influencer marketing to build brand awareness and engage with our target audience?
101. Can you create an influencer marketing campaign that aligns with our overall marketing goals and objectives?
102. How can we use data analysis to identify the most effective influencers for our brand?

103. How can we use influencer marketing to generate leads and drive conversions?
104. How can we use influencer marketing to improve our online reputation and credibility?

105. **Content creation**
106. How can we create high-quality content that resonates with our target audience and drives engagement?
107. Can you create a content creation strategy that aligns with our overall marketing goals and objectives?
108. How can we use data analysis to inform our content creation strategy and improve its effectiveness?
109. How can we use storytelling to improve the effectiveness of our content and build brand loyalty?
110. How can we use user-generated content to improve our content and build community?

111. **Email marketing**
112. How can we use email marketing to generate leads and drive conversions?
113. Can you create an email marketing campaign that aligns with our overall marketing goals and objectives?

114. How can we use data analysis to measure the effectiveness of our email marketing campaigns and make informed decisions?
115. How can we use persuasive language and calls-to-action to improve the effectiveness of our email marketing campaigns?
116. How can we use segmentation and personalization to improve the effectiveness of our email marketing campaigns?

117. **User experience design**
118. How can we improve our website's user experience to improve engagement and drive conversions?
119. Can you create a user experience design strategy that aligns with our overall marketing goals and objectives?
120. How can we use data analysis to identify areas for improvement in our website's user experience?
121. How can we use persuasive design elements to improve the effectiveness of our website's user experience?
122. How can we use A/B testing to measure the effectiveness of our user experience design strategy and make informed decisions?

123. Search engine optimization (SEO)

124. How can we improve our website's search engine ranking to increase organic traffic?
125. Can you create an SEO strategy that aligns with our overall marketing goals and objectives?
126. How can we use data analysis to identify keywords and optimize our website's content for search engines?
127. How can we use link building to improve our [website's authority] and search engine ranking?
128. How can we use local SEO to improve our visibility in local search results?

129. Pay-per-click (PPC) advertising

130. How can we use PPC advertising to generate leads and drive conversions?
131. Can you create a PPC advertising campaign that aligns with our overall marketing goals and objectives?
132. How can we use data analysis to measure the effectiveness of our PPC advertising campaigns and make informed decisions?
133. How can we use persuasive language and calls-to-action to improve the effectiveness of our PPC advertising campaigns?

134. How can we use segmentation and targeting to improve the effectiveness of our PPC advertising campaigns?

135. **Conversion rate optimization (CRO)**
136. How can we improve our website's conversion rate to drive more sales and revenue?
137. Can you create a CRO strategy that aligns with our overall marketing goals and objectives?
138. How can we use data analysis to identify areas for improvement in our website's conversion rate?
139. How can we use persuasive design elements to improve the effectiveness of our website's conversion rate?
140. How can we use A/B testing to measure the effectiveness of our CRO strategy and make informed decisions?

141. **Customer relationship management (CRM)**
142. How can we use CRM software to manage customer interactions and improve customer retention?
143. Can you recommend a CRM software that aligns with our business needs and objectives?

144. How can we use data analysis to segment our customer base and personalize our interactions with them?
145. How can we use automation to streamline our customer interactions and improve efficiency?
146. How can we use customer feedback to improve our products and services and build brand loyalty?

147. **Business strategy**
148. How can we develop a business strategy that aligns with our long-term goals and objectives?
149. Can you conduct a SWOT analysis to identify our business's strengths, weaknesses, opportunities, and threats?
150. How can we use data analysis to inform our business strategy and make informed decisions?
151. How can we use strategic planning to prioritize our goals and initiatives?
152. How can we use performance metrics to measure the effectiveness of our business strategy and make adjustments as needed?

153. **Market research**
154. How can we conduct market research to better understand our target audience and competition?

155. Can you create a market research plan that aligns with our business goals and objectives?
156. How can we use data analysis to interpret and make decisions based on market research data?
157. How can we use user testing to validate our assumptions and gather feedback on our products and services?
158. How can we use market research to inform our pricing strategy and product development?

159. **Financial management**
160. How can we improve our financial management practices to increase profitability and efficiency?
161. Can you create a financial management plan that aligns with our business goals and objectives?
162. How can we use financial data analysis to identify areas for cost savings and revenue growth?
163. How can we use budgeting and forecasting to plan for future growth and potential risks?
164. How can we use financial reporting to track our progress and make informed decisions?

165. **Supply chain management**
166. How can we improve our supply chain management practices to increase efficiency and reduce costs?

167. Can you create a supply chain management plan that aligns with our business goals and objectives?
168. How can we use data analysis to identify areas for improvement in our supply chain management?
169. How can we use automation and technology to streamline our supply chain processes and improve efficiency?

170. **Human resources**
171. How can we improve our human resources practices to attract and retain top talent?
172. Can you create a human resources strategy that aligns with our business goals and objectives?
173. How can we use data analysis to identify areas for improvement in our human resources practices?
174. How can we use performance management to measure and improve employee performance?
175. How can we use employee engagement strategies to improve employee satisfaction and retention?

176. **Legal and regulatory compliance**
177. How can we ensure our business is in compliance with all relevant laws and regulations?
178. Can you conduct a legal and regulatory compliance audit to identify potential areas of risk?

179. How can we use technology to streamline legal and regulatory compliance processes?
180. How can we use risk management strategies to minimize legal and regulatory risks?
181. How can we stay up-to-date on changes to laws and regulations that impact our business?

182. **Intellectual property protection**
183. How can we protect our intellectual property (IP) and prevent infringement?
184. Can you conduct an IP audit to identify potential areas of risk?
185. How can we use legal strategies to protect our IP rights?
186. How can we use technology to monitor and detect potential infringement of our IP?
187. How can we use IP licensing and partnerships to generate additional revenue?

188. **Branding and identity**
189. How can we develop a strong brand identity that resonates with our target audience?
190. Can you create a branding strategy that aligns with our business goals and objectives?

191. How can we use design and visual elements to create a consistent brand identity?
192. How can we use messaging and storytelling to communicate our brand values and mission?
193. How can we measure the effectiveness of our branding strategy and make adjustments as needed?

194. **Content marketing**
195. How can we use content marketing to attract and engage our target audience?
196. Can you create a content marketing plan that aligns with our business goals and objectives?
197. How can we use data analysis to identify topics and formats that resonate with our target audience?
198. How can we use content distribution strategies to reach our target audience across multiple channels?
199. How can we measure the effectiveness of our content marketing efforts and make adjustments as needed?

200. **Social media marketing**
201. How can we use social media to reach and engage our target audience?
202. Can you create a social media marketing plan that aligns with our business goals and objectives?

203. How can we use data analysis to identify social media platforms and content formats that resonate with our target audience?
204. How can we use social media advertising to reach a larger audience and drive conversions?
205. How can we measure the effectiveness of our social media marketing efforts and make adjustments as needed?

206. **Email marketing**
207. How can we use email marketing to nurture leads and drive conversions?
208. Can you create an email marketing plan that aligns with our business goals and objectives?
209. How can we use data analysis to segment our email list and personalize our communications?
210. How can we use email automation to streamline our communications and improve efficiency?
211. How can we measure the effectiveness of our email marketing efforts and make adjustments as needed?

212. **Influencer marketing**
213. How can we use influencer marketing to reach and engage our target audience?

214. Can you create an influencer marketing plan that aligns with our business goals and objectives?
215. How can we use data analysis to identify influencers that align with our brand values and mission?
216. How can we use influencer partnerships to generate additional revenue and reach a larger audience?
217. How can we measure the effectiveness of our influencer marketing efforts and make adjustments as needed?

218. Affiliate marketing

219. How can we use affiliate marketing to generate additional revenue and reach a larger audience?
220. Can you create an affiliate marketing plan that aligns with our business goals and objectives?
221. How can we use data analysis to identify affiliate partners that align with our brand values and mission?
222. How can we use affiliate partnerships to drive conversions and increase customer loyalty?
223. How can we measure the effectiveness of our affiliate marketing efforts and make adjustments as needed?

224. **E-commerce optimization**
225. How can we improve our e-commerce website to drive conversions and increase revenue?
226. Can you conduct an e-commerce website audit to identify potential areas for improvement?
227. How can we use user experience design to create a seamless shopping experience for our customers?
228. How can we use data analysis to optimize our product offerings and pricing strategies?
229. How can we measure the effectiveness of our e-commerce optimization efforts and make adjustments as needed?

230. **Customer service**
231. How can we improve our customer service practices to increase customer satisfaction and retention?
232. Can you create a customer service strategy that aligns with our business goals and objectives?
233. How can we use technology to improve our customer service efficiency and effectiveness?
234. How can we use data analysis to identify areas for improvement in our customer service practices?
235. How can we measure the effectiveness of our customer service efforts and make adjustments as needed?

236. **Crisis management**
237. How can we develop a crisis management plan to respond to potential crises or emergencies?
238. Can you conduct a risk assessment to identify potential areas of risk?
239. How can we use communication strategies to keep our stakeholders informed and engaged during a crisis?
240. How can we use technology to streamline our crisis management processes and improve efficiency?
241. How can we measure the effectiveness of our crisis management efforts and make adjustments as needed?

ABOUT THE AUTHOR

David Dada is not merely a tech consultant; he is a confluence where technology, financial acumen, and innovative digital solutions seamlessly intertwine. With a career spanning over two decades, David has carved a niche for himself in various tech-related domains, including but not limited to Banking, Accounting, Fullstack Programming, Information Security, Smart Contract development, and Media. His expansive knowledge and aptitude for marrying technology with practical, client-focused solutions have catapulted him into a realm where digital advancement is not just observed but actively sculpted.

As the Co-founder and CEO of The Digital Tribes Technology Limited, and the esteemed President and Chairman of the Board of Trustees of the Digital Tribes Cooperative, a forward-thinking FinTech Cooperative, David is ceaselessly steering the ship towards uncharted territories in the digital world, uncovering novel ways of integrating technological advancements with pragmatic solutions in the financial sector. "Generative AI: Unleashing Creative Genius with Prompt Engineering" is not just a testament to his profound knowledge in the tech realm but is also a beacon, illuminating the path for aspiring tech enthusiasts, professionals, and novices alike, guiding them through the intricacies of prompt engineering in AI, with the finesse that only a seasoned professional like David could weave.

www.ingramcontent.com/pod-product-compliance
Lightning Source LLC
Chambersburg PA
CBHW052200220526
45471CB00004B/1748